Charles H. Horton
RAMC
21 October 189
19 October 19

Compiled and edited b
Dale le Vack

STRETCHER
BEARER!

Fighting for life
in the trenches

LION

Published by Lion Books
an imprint of
Lion Hudson plc
Wilkinson House, Jordan Hill Road,
Oxford OX2 8DR, England
www.lionhudson.com/lion

ISBN 978 0 7459 5566 7
e-ISBN 978 0 7459 5711 1

First edition 2013

Picture acknowledgments
Front cover, spine and p. 3: Portait of Charles H. Horton and inset of camp used by
kind permission of Charles Horton's daughter, Eileen Mary Emerson.
Cover: Stretcher bearers: Corbis/Bettman; handwritten letter: iStockphoto/andipantz;
envelopes and stamps: iStockphoto/Hande Yuce; aged paper: iStockphoto/Kim Sohee;
stained paper: iStockphoto/Aleksey Tkachenko.
pp. 12, 32–33, 53, 122: Family photographs are used by kind permission of Eileen
Mary Emersen.
Text acknowledgments
Every effort has been made to trace the original copyright holders where required. In
some cases this has proved impossible. We shall be happy to correct any such omissions
in future editions.
p. 70: Extract copyright © Siegfried Sassoon reprinted by kind permission of the Estate
of George Sassoon.
pp. 139–41, 154–55: Noel Chavasse correspondence reprinted by permission of the
Chavasse family.
pp. 155–64: Thomas Fred Littler's diary reprinted by permission of www.first-world-
war-co.uk

A catalogue record for this book is available from the British Library

Printed and bound in the UK, August 2014, LH26

CONTENTS

INTRODUCTION: THE ROYAL ARMY MEDICAL CORPS

The Royal Army Medical Corps (RAMC) has been responsible for medical care in the British Army since 1898. The need for a specialist internal unit for treating soldiers and returning them speedily to active service has long been recognized. Visit a Roman fort in Britain, for example, Housesteads on Hadrian's Wall, and you will see the outline of a building thought to have been a form of hospital or infirmary for sick and injured Roman soldiers.

Medical services within the British army can be traced back to the formation of the standing regular army following the restoration of Charles II in 1660, when regimental surgeons began to be appointed. Failings were exposed during active service and the need for drastic improvements became obvious, leading to changes. Major problems emerged during the Napoleonic campaigns and, particularly, the Crimean War of 1854–56.

Towards the end of the nineteenth century there was considerable pressure for change within the army's medical services. This pressure came largely from the British Medical Association, the corporate body of the medical profession. The BMA believed that the problems with medical care in the army were largely caused by the low status of doctors within the service. And so in 1898, the Royal Army Medical Corps was formed.

Perhaps the main advance was that RAMC medical staff were now accorded officer ranks the same as those in the wider army, giving them an authoritative voice they may have lacked before. The RAMC was soon tested to the limit, during the Boer War of 1899–1902. An RAMC college was set up, with its new building inaugurated at Millbank in London in 1907, and the RAMC was also modified, along with the rest of the army, during the Haldane reforms in the years that followed. The outbreak of the First World War in 1914 presented the RAMC with unprecedented challenges.

It will be useful here to explain one aspect of RAMC terminology. Horton served in an RAMC field ambulance, and this is perhaps a slightly misleading term for us today. A field ambulance was not a vehicle but rather a large and diverse unit that operated a number of medical facilities just behind the front line, as will become clear in Horton's story. During the First World War, vehicles for transporting the wounded were usually referred to as motor ambulances.

RAMC officers were armed, but were only entitled to use those arms in self-defence. RAMC stretcher bearers were unarmed. The unit was not a fighting unit, yet during the First World War its personnel saw at least as much of the horror of conflict as did the fighting troops, and nearly 7,000 of them became casualties. The RAMC's motto is *In Arduis Fidelis*, which is Latin for "Faithful in Adversity". The experiences of the RAMC in that war are summed up in a poem, entitled "The R.A.M.C.", written by Corporal W.H. Atkins (A Coy, 1/8th Worcestershire Regiment):

> *We carry no rifle, bayonet nor bomb,*
> *But follow behind in rear*
> *Of the steel fringed line that surges along*
> *With a ringing British cheer.*
> *Through the tangled wire of the blown-in trench,*
> *Spite of shrapnel or bursting shell,*
> *We make for the spots – Khaki-clad helpless blots –*
> *That mark where our front rank fell.*

We are the men who carry them back,
The wounded, the dying and dead.
It's "Halt!" "Dressing Here!" – "Come, buck up, old dear,"
You're all right for "Blighty," so be of good cheer –
"Turn him gently now, bandage his head."
The "stretcher-bearers" doing their bit,
Of V.C.s, not many they score,
Yet are earned every day in a quiet sort of way
By the "Royal Army Medical Corps".

IN ARDUIS FIDELIS

Never for them the awful joy
That sets the soldier's breast afire,
The lust to conquer and destroy,
The blazing passion, mad desire;
Spurred by no glory to be won,
Not warmed by battle's heated breath,
Only a sad task to be done,
They do their duty – true till death.

Denied the pomp and pride of war,
The peril alone is theirs to share;
Yet, self and safety flung afar,
They do what mortal men may dare.
Steadfast in their Christ-given faith,
All for others, if need, they give;
Faithful in danger, true till death,
They die that fellow-men may live.

I

INTRODUCING CHARLES HERBERT "BERT" HORTON

This is a book about a non-combatant in the front line in the First World War who was there not to kill men but to save them. It has been published, long after the death of its author, as a testimony to ordinary men like him who were in the armed forces during the First World War. He set out to explain in his memoirs what it was like to be an ordinary bloke serving as a stretcher bearer in the army during the conflict.

When he wrote about his war, Private Charles Herbert Horton (2305), who served on the Western Front and in Italy, wanted to record for posterity the everyday life of men who volunteered for service and endured the dangerous but often tedious army life on active service, usually without recognition – apart perhaps from a service medal or two. Private Horton was entitled to wear the Victory Medal and the British War Medal but there is no record that he ever bothered to apply for them.

These memoirs are historically valuable because they are among the few personal accounts published about men from the ranks. He writes:

*There is an almost complete absence of any
personal history of the many thousands who
exchanged civvies for khaki to serve in the ranks,
to do as authority told them and to accept the
ordeal of deadly danger, rough conditions and
some ineffable boredom for month after month
and year after year, and who were still lucky
enough to survive to the end.*

Charles Herbert Horton, known to his family as Bert, was a
19-year-old graduate when he joined the RAMC. He came from
a deeply Christian middle-class family living in Handsworth,
Birmingham, and he attended Handsworth Grammar School,
where he was a scholar. His name is to be seen in the school
register in the entrance hall. At the outbreak of the war he was

Charles's father and mother, Joseph and Harriet Horton

about to enter his third year of studies for a degree in commerce at Birmingham University.

Joseph and Harriet Horton brought up their three children, Nellie, Bert, and Joseph Arthur to have Nonconformist religious beliefs.[1] Joseph was a preacher on a Methodist circuit[2] for much of his life and was associated for thirty years with Asbury Memorial Wesleyan Church, Handsworth, in which he was leader of the Young Men's Bible Class. In fact he held every office open to a layman. A keen musician, Joseph was a flautist and a member of the Birmingham Choral and Orchestral Society. Bert's brother, Arthur, became organist at Perry Barr Wesleyan Church.

Bert, an accomplished violinist, inherited from Joseph a strong personal distaste for conventional soldiering, because it would involve him in killing men. He was patriotic, however, and so, after getting his degree in 1915, he opted to volunteer to join the corps in the British Army that was dedicated to saving life rather than taking it – and he did so as a stretcher bearer prepared to serve overseas in front-line duty.

He was also prepared to set aside the possibility of obtaining a commission to which his education had prepared him, because in the Royal Army Medical Corps (RAMC) these were reserved exclusively for doctors, dentists, and other professional specialists in the field of medicine. In any case, being an officer in the RAMC would have meant carrying firearms and learning to use other weaponry, a requirement for all who held the king's commission.

Instead, Bert served in the ranks of the corps and despite his education and intellect was content to remain a private soldier throughout his years in the army, even turning down the opportunity to become a non-commissioned officer. He seemed to want no part of the military command structure, preferring to remain in and around the front line – dedicated to saving life.

His intellect and bilingual skills were finally recognized at the end of the war when he was selected to be a member of a British Army delegation from the RAMC to travel to Vienna, whose mission was the safe return of British prisoners of war.

He came from a generation taught not to express emotion or pass on to others the full horror and butchery of warfare in the trenches, for example, in his letters home. Censorship also ensured he could not do so in these letters. It was expected of young men from a Nonconformist background that they should be modest in both thought and expression. This was the kind of man that Bert Horton was. It comes through clearly in his writing. He told his family that unless illness prevented it, he never missed chapel on a Sunday, even while he served on or near the front line.

In this book the vivid horrors of war are left largely for others to imagine. There are no passages that describe in shocking or dramatic detail what he witnessed in the battlefield. He never tells us of the distress, pity, or revulsion he must have felt at the sights, sounds, and smell of the dead and the soon to die.

Bert Horton knew that death stalked him and his comrades: the fear of it, the horrific sight of shattered bodies, the screams of the dying and the constant shelling. However, we never hear about the physical ordeal of carrying a human being across bog-ridden terrain, the mud, the biting cold and endless drizzle, the disgusting nature of dressing wounds that may have turned septic or been spewing puss. Yet he was familiar with them all in the heat of battle in the advanced dressing stations to which he brought the wounded.

He seems to have preferred that his personal account of the war should sound ordinary, even humdrum. Of course, it was not, but we can only speculate the underlying reason for understatement. It may be that the mental effort required in recalling in detail the horrors he witnessed in the written word was just too painful for an old man. Perhaps he could not bear to relive them. One of the stated reasons for Bert Horton writing his memoirs is protest.

In the aftermath of battle, the RAMC stretcher bearers – as opposed to regimental stretcher bearers – rarely received official recognition for what they had done in the shelling zone where they were usually based. None of the RAMC men awarded the Victoria Cross were stretcher bearers from the ranks. They were all officer doctors.

Several VCs, however, were awarded to regimental stretcher bearers who accompanied combatants into action. These men were ordinary soldiers who had volunteered to augment and work alongside regimental bandsmen, who traditionally did the job on the battlefield. Unlike RAMC stretcher bearers they were also trained to carry and use firearms.

Regimental stretcher bearers were more likely to win medals for conspicuous gallantry than RAMC stretcher bearers, not necessarily because they were more courageous, but because they worked primarily from the regimental aid posts and were right on the front line – and were required to venture into no-man's-land alongside the fighting men.

By contrast, for much of the time (there were many exceptions), the RAMC stretcher bearers were positioned behind the immediate area of no-man's-land, taking the wounded to the advanced aid posts. In this area, just to the rear of each of the opposing armies, stretcher bearers were often exposed to continuous shell-fire, but less often to bullets and bombs thrown at close range.

Many RAMC stretcher bearers, including Bert Horton, believed that their war service went largely unrecognized because they did not (and in some cases were not prepared to) bear arms against the enemy. However, no official documents have ever come to light that would confirm this suspicion.

Significantly, after 1916 the RAMC was the chosen corps of thousands of men who refused to fight under any circumstances – the registered conscientious objectors or "conchies" as they were known.

The popular belief that "conchies" were at heart cowards was exacerbated because the post-1916 conscientious objectors were not volunteers – as Horton was – but conscripted men who were required by law to fight for king and country. Many "absolutists" – as some conscientious objectors were known – were imprisoned for refusing even to wear the army uniform and to participate in any form in the war effort. They were marked men, deemed unemployable, for many years after the war when they returned to civilian life.

There were exceptions when a gallantry medal was awarded to an RAMC stretcher bearer who was registered as a conscientious objector. Private Ernest Gregory was a conscientious objector who refused to fight, but he was also a volunteer in the corps, like Bert Horton had been. Gregory "the conchie" – as he was called – won the Military Medal in 1917 during the Battle of Passchendaele. The citation reads:

> *Pte Gregory of the 1/3rd West Riding Field Ambulance RAMC was awarded his medal for conspicuous bravery in the field for bringing in wounded men in terrible conditions – under fire and through shell holes and mud-filled water up to the armpits.*

Although Bert Horton does not reveal in detail the acts of heroism he himself and other private soldiers performed, or actually witnessed, during the summer of 1916 and later in 1917, it is clear that acts of conspicuous bravery, often carried out on the spur of the moment, were taking place all around him – both during the Battle of the Somme and in the Third Battle of Ypres at Passchendaele.

Books and films about the Great War have shown that acts of spontaneous bravery by unsung heroes that might have resulted in gallantry awards took place every day, but were not recognized or recalled in the aftermath of combat, sometimes because no one was left alive to validate them.

At the same time, it would be incorrect to claim that stretcher bearers serving in the RAMC were never recognized for their gallantry in the field – because 3,002 non-commissioned officers and other ranks in the corps received the Military Medal between 1914 and 1918, some with bars. However, the award of the Distinguished Conduct Medal, the Military Medal, and other gallantry awards to other ranks in the RAMC constitutes well under 2 per cent of the 120,000 men and women who served in the corps during 1914–18.

Bravery awards in the First World War were the result of an administrative route which began with the act of conspicuous bravery itself. The system started with someone considered of responsibility witnessing an act and reporting it into the chain of command. At each reported stage, consideration was given to taking it a stage further. Assuming that the full consideration path was followed, the stage was reached where someone in the command structure had the job of confirming the award or denying it.

In old age in the 1970s Horton, who as we know was not a registered conscientious objector, argues that the RAMC is possibly the most overlooked of all branches of the services – rarely referenced by war writers or war records. Humble and modest men like Private Bert Horton of the RAMC remained in the shadows of military existence.

One can detect in Horton's writing over half a century later a sense of frustration that public interest in the Great War appeared to have diminished significantly as he became an old man. Bert Horton did not live long enough to witness the revival in the public appetite for publications, both factual and fictionalized, about the First World War.

The outbreak of the First World War in August 1914 is now perceived correctly as the setting from which many of the traumatic events of a troubled century sprang during successive decades. The question remains whether the young generation of the early twenty-first century will learn from it. Bert Horton tells us:

> *Not all the war memorials and Armistice Day Festivals can pay a tithe to the tribute due to those whose lot it was to be offered up as cannon fodder in this most bloody of all campaigns the world has seen.*

2

1970: REFLECTIONS ON A CONFLICT

EXTRACTS FROM BERT HORTON'S DIARIES
Over several decades in the twentieth century, a generation grew up who knew little of the anniversaries of the historic episodes of the Great War, such as on 1 July 1916, the first day of the Battle of the Somme. We surviving combatants who served in the trenches in the Great War, now old men, usually felt a sense of reluctance to speak or write about any of the events connected with it, except perhaps the beginning and the end.

Whether the opening day of the Battle of the Somme is one of those events which the student of history, long after my generation has faded away, will ultimately be required to remember, is perhaps debatable.

Nevertheless, it is certain that for the dwindling numbers of us left, the date 1 July 1916 and the four and a half months that followed it, will continue to recall ineffaceable personal memories – as full of emotion as any other date on the calendar, even Armistice Day.

To hundreds of thousands of veterans in all parts of the earth it must always be a day of mourning – for probably on no other single day were so many brave men sent to eternity. They were our band of brothers, whose young lives were cut short.

"Between the rising and setting of one summer sun" as the late Conan Doyle put it, more than 100,000 British, French, Commonwealth, and German combatants became casualties. To those of us who took part in the battle and survived it, the memories of our individual experiences return as vividly after the passage of the years as they ever did. For all this horror the memories have something of grandeur in them which makes us a little sorry, maybe, for those of later generations who may have nothing so vivid to remember.

It is not my intention to recall once more the heroism of the men who went over the top in the great bid for victory, nor do I wish to portray the horrors which my job of Royal Army Medical Corps stretcher bearer gave me a special opportunity to witness. To paint either aspect of the picture more adequately than it has been done before is beyond my powers. The published accounts, which exist from the pens of eyewitnesses and others, make salutary reading. In the following pages, I have set down most of what I remember of the experiences of myself and my ambulance unit in the two and a half remaining years of the war and the months of waiting for release from service.

I want to answer the question why I have troubled, after the lapse of half a century, to set down this record. I think that the urge came upon me in retirement and ripe old age, partly because of the conviction that history is the sum total of the experiences of individuals.

As we learnt it, history is the story of the exalted ones and their ambitions and their rivalries, of governments and kings, of international diplomacy, of the strategy of wars, the causes of victory and defeat. The wars were fought by professional soldiers. The two great wars of the twentieth century were waged mainly by civilians-turned-soldiers.

The Second World War, involving as it did for the first time in this country the people at home in the savagery of destruction, also took place in an era when press reportage and photography had advanced enormously. Journalists were able to give the world authentic records of the stark realities of the struggle thanks to the toleration and even encouragement from the brass-hats.

In all my 1916–18 war service, I never saw a press reporter, not a camera, still less a cine-camera. The pictures I have since seen in contemporary newspapers – there were far more from the French front than the British – had been taken miles behind the lines and, more often than not, had been selectively produced to boost home morale. These featured the sight of long lines of German prisoners being escorted by smiling British "Tommies". To visit the Imperial War Museum now is to get the impression that the 1914–18 war is already ancient history of which the available relics are specimens of old weapons, gas-masks and uniforms and a few pictures of battered French and Belgian towns.

As for written records, there are books aplenty on the origins of the war, the rights and wrongs of what the politicians and the generals did, and what the war cost in money and human life. True, there have been graphic accounts by professional writers and notabilities on their personal experiences, generally as infantry officers, often of short duration.

There is, however, an almost complete absence of any personal history of the many thousands who exchanged civvies for khaki to serve in the ranks, to do as authority told them and to accept the ordeal of deadly danger, rough conditions and some ineffable boredom for month after month and year after year, and who were still lucky enough to survive to the end.

The Medical Corps can surely claim to be the most widely ignored of all branches of the services, ignored by organizers of small town Remembrance Day Parades, seldom referred to by any writers whose accounts of personal experiences have found their way into libraries, or those who have sought to piece together the progress of warfare from available records. Today, many adults and most schoolchildren, would find difficulty in recalling what the initials RAMC stood for.

There are many ramifications to the Army Medical Services, on many of which a mere member of a field ambulance is unqualified to speak. One of my friends who came out later than myself to the forward area in France found himself allotted duties temporarily at a base hospital near the coast, which happened to be a VD hospital. He had first-hand experience of one of the other services performed by the RAMC, and from his accounts it was an experience which I have always been heartily thankful to have missed.

I am prepared to accept that there were many safe jobs where duties were continually arduous, often distasteful, and deserving of grateful acknowledgement. However, the work of the field ambulances can claim to fall into a different category. Non-combatant we may have been, but we were well up among the most fully involved combatants. Our normal field of operations was between the field artillery and the infantry.

The aid posts in which we lived and were on call, night and day, were in this area and the individuals manning these posts normally remained there for the duration of occupancy of the sector of the brigade, not the battalions in the brigade, which were moved from reserve to support and thence to front-line duty in rotation.

If RAMC stretcher bearers were sometimes spared the hazards of short-range missiles, the bullet and hand-grenade and the shell-fire concentrated on the front trenches, except for the time required to pick up stretcher cases to carry away, no one with experience of trench warfare would deny that the area I have roughly defined, *stretching a mile or more behind the firing line could be, and often was, extremely unhealthy.*

What my unit experienced in France and Belgium, on the Somme and later in the salient at Passchendaele, was almost entirely stationary warfare, in which most of the sacrifices in lives of the fighting men were made without gain of territory or other advantage. All this must be laid at the door of those in high places whose minds could conceive of no better way of conducting operations. Not all the war memorials and Armistice Day festivals can pay a tithe to the tribute due to those whose lot it was to be offered up as cannon fodder in this most bloody of all campaigns the world has seen.

But for the fact that many RAMC men gave their lives or suffered wounds in the course of their duty, no great injustice would be done if only the infantry were remembered in history. If non-combatant contributions are to be given a place in the picture at all, my humble submission is that the RAMC stretcher bearers should be there.

3

EUROPE VIOLATED

The day war breaks out in August 1914, I am on holiday with my family at Colwyn Bay in North Wales. It is my last long vacation from Birmingham University to which I am due to return for my third year of studies. I look upon the future with confidence. All being well, my university studies will enable me to emerge into the big world with a degree in commerce to start a career. I have no plans beyond that and am content to see what the future might offer.

I am two months short of 19 years of age, having been admitted to the university two years earlier only by special dispensation, the minimum age for admission according to the rules being 17. From the beach, we see trains full of khaki-clad troops passing along that coastal route from Holyhead and no doubt from Ireland. We watch them with detachment, unaware that the world is changing forever in front of our eyes.

To be at war is certainly regrettable, but we feel it is something to be dealt with by our army and navy. At this early stage there is no sense of historic catastrophe or impending disaster. Apart from colonial wars and then the Crimea and Boer Wars there has been no threat of any sort to our way of life for 100 years.

Britain's armed forces have proved fully equal to all previous demands made of it – and could surely be trusted to demonstrate once again that the might of the British Empire is unassailable. Surely this bid to conquer territory by the Kaiser will be dealt with by Christmas and the international status quo and peace restored throughout Europe.

We finish our fortnight's holiday and return to our home in Stafford Road, Handsworth. We are entirely dependent at this time on the newspapers for information and day by day it becomes more and more apparent that our forces have come up against more serious opposition than has ever been encountered before.

We understand our small regular army has to be augmented, and quickly, and that we should respond to the government's call for volunteers. The brilliant performance of the British Expeditionary Force at Mons in Belgium and the heroic stand by Frenchmen and Englishmen on the Marne shows that the rapacious Hun can be checked.

As the government's call becomes more urgent it is supported from all quarters, particularly the press, the theatres, even the churches, and the response to its demands come from young men in every walk of life.

I hear of one school friend after another who is enlisting. I have not been a member of the Officers' Training Corps at Handsworth Grammar School, nor of that at the university. At school, the consent of my father Joseph Horton to my joining is requested but declined, and I make no objection as I have no great urge to be taught the use of lethal weapons and the art of leadership in war.

Frankly, I find the sight of some of my fellow pupils in uniform, and some of the masters too, rather ridiculous – particularly when being drilled by the caretaker, an ex-regular, now elevated to the role of sergeant major. However, we are all two years older than when I left school, and the OTC boys are now being accepted for commissions. I begin to feel a sense of isolation, yet my Nonconformist environment makes me wary of regarding the actions of the majority as necessarily right for me.

I know my father has made great sacrifices to pay for my continued education and the only return I can make to him is to finish the course and get my degree, or at least take my final exams. This will take nine months, or eight, counting from the time I will have attained official enlistment age. Finally, I decide to stay and if the war still continues in June 1915 offer myself for war service immediately after the exams are over.

So, in the space of a few weeks, I am back in the lecture room, now as a third-year undergraduate intent on making a good job of the final stage of the course, but increasingly aware that it is much more likely to lead straight into war service than the career which has hitherto been the goal.

A few of our contemporaries have already joined up and we hear from time to time news of men who have graduated in the previous June and are now already in action, some already casualties. Former colleagues on short leave drop in from time to time to visit us, usually in the uniform of subaltern. Our German lecturer, whose faulty English has often given us occasion for unseemly mirth, is understood to be fighting as an officer on the other side and the English professor in the same subject is, we hear, in British Intelligence.

So with the stark realities of outside life always in our minds, we continue the routine of lectures, home studies, common-room conversations, and exams until finals come around. Enlistment is still voluntary and so is choice of Service.

I decide to opt for the Royal Army Medical Corps, volunteering for the 1st South Midland Field Ambulance, which is based in barracks on Great Brook Street in Birmingham. I know little about the corps, but from friends who have already joined am convinced that service in a field ambulance offers me what I want: full involvement in the risks and hardships which the rest of my generation has accepted, without the obligation to take life.

On my first attempt at enlistment, I am told that recruitment is temporarily suspended but that I will be informed immediately it is resumed. So, one fine day when I am taking a leisurely walk in the park, which is near my home in Handsworth, a figure in private's uniform, whom I do not know, but who knows my friend at the same RAMC Barracks, seeks and finds me, apparently without difficulty.

"Are you Charles Horton?" he asks.

"Yes, that's me," I reply.

"I have come to tell you that you can now report to the barracks and should do so without delay," he advises.

This short delay in my enlistment would not be worth recording but that James, himself a new volunteer and soon to be a close friend, is to be one of my companions on the first draft to be sent six months later to the "first line" of the ambulance in France.[3] After another six months he is to be the first of our number to be killed – on his first night in the trenches – when I am immediately behind him and separated by not more than a yard.

The first line of the field ambulance, a unit in which I enlist, is a territorial unit attached to the South Midland Division. Most of the members of the field ambulance have, of course, been together for training in peacetime. The draft of a dozen or so recruits, of which I am one, is the first to join the unit and the first leaven of wartime volunteers to be added to this group of Saturday afternoon soldiers.

They are already well acquainted with one another, including the NCOs and warrant officers promoted from the ranks. In one respect, we start on level terms in that the unit has not yet been called upon to serve in action. On the other hand, they have become fully accustomed to living conditions for troops behind the line.

For me, the time spent in training in England is a nine-till-five job: going into barracks by tram in the morning from home, where I am officially billeted, and back to freedom in the evenings. The exception is when we spend six weeks at the end of the summer in camp near Warwick, and even from here I have at least one weekend leave.

We are billeted at a barracks in Birmingham where we do our square-bashing drills and route marches out of the town to places as distant as Castle Bromwich and Frankley Waterworks. We endure with good humour the physical jerks and the seemingly senseless exercises with stretchers which take the place of infantry skill at arms drill. All these exercises increase our physical fitness and inure us to military discipline, while lectures on elementary physiology and first aid provide, as well as relaxation and some amusement, a little specialized knowledge to boost our morale.

The spell under canvas in late summer 1915 introduces us to the more rigorous aspects of soldiering. These are the days before we are issued with infantry packs and we march from the station at Warwick, where we have previously been kitted out with uniforms and all paraphernalia down to one hussif,[4] one lanyard, and a jack knife.

Our overcoats are rolled and slung, bandolier-fashion, over one shoulder and the tightly packed kit-bag, balanced awkwardly and with growing discomfort, on the other. We find our field camp at Wedgnock in the rolling Warwickshire countryside and discover our bell-tents are already pitched. In each of these six of us sleep with feet to the pole. There is nothing between us and the uneven field but ground sheets and nothing between our flesh and the army blankets but our army underwear.

We are introduced to army food, cooked in "dixies" over a trench fire and served into our mess tins, which has to serve both for stew at midday and tea in the evening, with nothing but cold water, straw and mud to remove the grease and the distinctive flavour of Maconochie's meat and vegetable ration.

We wash at an ablution bench with cold water from a standpipe, scrounge hot water for shaving where we can, and relieve ourselves in the pole-and-bucket latrines tactically disposed at the edge of the meadow and screened by hessian. We do physical jerks before breakfast, but are fortified at a later stage with hot black coffee. We are paraded later in front of our tents with blankets neatly folded and equipment laid out for inspection.

Of course, we continue with our drilling and marching but now under the eye of a martinet of a sergeant major, decked out in a uniform so closely resembling that of a commissioned officer that he receives, but does not acknowledge, salutes all over the place from infantrymen from neighbouring camps.

We have, of course, already determined our attitudes to the different NCOs we have met so far and I think these can be summed up as generally critical, but never really hostile. However, this new agent of authority inspires nothing but repugnance and we begin to see in the prospect of service in France at least one attractive feature; deliverance from pettifogging discipline.

It is while here that I have what can be called my first experience of "nursing", though of a sort which, happily is never repeated. This is to take charge during a long night with an infantryman with "DTs" brought on by excessive alcohol, who awaits us lying on a wooden palette bed in a bell-tent, lit by a hurricane lantern. I have as companion in this weird vigil, a young recruit whose mental and physical equipment appears wholly inadequate to the situation and he makes no conversation, cheerful or otherwise.

Our patient, in his more active moments, roundly abuses us, gets up, and tries to find the keyhole in the front door of the tent. He also has to make sure there is nobody under his bed, which *is three inches above the ground. Towards morning he becomes more and more restless and anxious to get out.*

At breakfast time, we are relieved by a pair of men which include a very large, muscular individual who in civilian life has been an attendant at a lunatic asylum. He takes in the situation and at once demonstrates the "professional" way to handle it. The manner in which he makes the patient lie down seems a bit rough, but before we leave all is peace and quiet, the befuddled infantryman almost back to his senses and interested in food.

Soon after we have returned to barracks, the names are announced of those who are to form the first draft for the first line in France. They include all who have joined up before me and a few who arrive a little later, so that I have the satisfaction of the continued company of all who have become my close friends.

We are kitted out with more items of equipment, including the white armbands – brassards – bearing a red cross, to be worn on active service. On our own initiative we take the wire out of our hats which stretch the crown out flat like a drum. We expect to be away before Christmas 1915 but in the event it is not until the very last days of the old year that the summons comes.

RAMC Field camp. Bert Horton – far right (sitting).

4

ARRIVAL IN FRANCE

Prologue

For most of the First World War, the 1st South Midland Field Ambulance, in which Horton served, was attached to the 48th (South Midland) Division. This was a division of the Territorial Force (TF) created by the army reforms of Richard Burdon Haldane, who was Secretary of State for War between 1905 and 1912. One of fourteen divisions in the peacetime TF, the 48th Division incorporated twelve infantry battalions covering the counties of Berkshire, Buckinghamshire, Gloucestershire, Oxfordshire, Warwickshire, and Worcestershire in three brigades, including a South Midland Brigade.

The 48th Division was sent to the Western Front in March 1915 where it took part in the Battle of the Somme and the Battle of Pozières in 1916 and the Third Battle of Ypres the following year. In November 1917, the Division was part of a British force sent to Italy to help support the Italian war effort, and took up positions along the River Piave. The Division served there until the Armistice and remained in Italy until it returned to Britain in 1919.

We cross the Channel at night from Southampton in January 1916 on a calm sea without incident, and after daylight sail up the Seine to Rouen, where we disembark to march to our dispersal camp.

I remember nothing of that first night in France except having to perform some duties in the mess hall, where the bare tables are scraped down after meals to remove the remains of the rather revolting food served to us.

Our first introduction to our sleeping quarters is in the type of barn which we soon come to know as the universal style of farm architecture in rural northern France – walls of wattle and daub and a roof supported by a trellis of rough-hewn timbers based in turn on low walls, topped by more timber and running from the main walls only so far as to leave a central aisle.

In the alcoves thus formed and on the straw laid upon the ground, it is indicated that we are to make our beds. The straw on the ground is not new – nor are the blankets with which we are issued. However, we have our groundsheets to put under us and our stout army underwear to serve us in the dual role of pyjamas and protect us from too intimate contact with our environment.

During our training, recruits have been lucky enough to sleep most of the time at home in our own beds, but a brief spell under canvas has taught us a few tricks in furtherance of personal comfort under adverse conditions. We know one good though surprising way to make a pillow. After laying out our boots on their sides with soles outwards and uppers almost meeting, we place our neatly folded trousers in between – and that is all.

There is one very disturbed night in the sleeping hut, when a man comes in late who must have been returning from leave and persists, before he falls into a drunken sleep, in giving a solo version of the more obscene songs which are later to become familiar, but which at that time make most of us squirm with a righteous desire to silence the singer.

As regards the disposal of the bits and pieces, such as shaving tackle, soap etc, which a soldier likes to have readily at hand, the obvious place appears to be the shelf provided by the aforementioned low party walls, but we get a timely warning about this from the more experienced. It appears that these shelves are regularly used by rats which share the billet and will consume anything edible while knocking off the rest of the obstacles in their path. Noting this advice and the further kindly warning that we might well feel the same rodents running over us, we compose ourselves to somewhat uneasy sleep, having first snuffed out the candles which provide our only illumination.

In the morning, we start adapting ourselves to the new community we have entered and the new way of life we now must accept. Sanitation and ablutions are primitive but having washed, shaved, and dressed, we join the flock for breakfast.

In the central open yard of another farm across the village's only street we queue for our daily bread ration, half a loaf, and with mess tin and ditto lid at the ready, have tea (ready milked and sugared) served with a ladle from a "dixie" into the mess tin.

On the open trench fire which has boiled the "dixie", bacon is sizzling in a large deep pan of fat and one is welcome to dip one's loaf of bread into this and, if one has an egg, to fry that to go with the bacon.

Food is consumed al fresco if weather permits, otherwise in the billet with the now folded blankets for a seat. Tables and chairs are, like beds, luxuries we manage to dispense with, both at that time and the rest of the duration of the war.

Leaving all tidy in the billet, we foregather with buttons, cap-badge, and boots polished, for the morning parade of our section. In training, this ceremony has usually been followed by some square-bashing, physical jerks, perhaps a lecture, or ridiculous manoeuvres known as stretcher drill or a route march. It is a pleasure to note that none of these appear to be customs observed in this unit on active service. Instead, the practice is to divide us into small groups for various fatigues.

The first order following inspection and any remarks the staff sergeant in charge sees fit to make to us is invariably "Fall out the sanitary men". These dedicated men depart apparently quite happily to their vital, if unsavoury, work and are no more to be seen.

From time to time the problem of finding jobs for men in a unit on rest as we technically are must be exacting. I have known it solved at various times with such different assignments as ditch-clearing, spring-cleaning farmyards and pigsties, and in Italy, tree-felling and stone-breaking. At this particular juncture, a task presents itself which solves the problem for quite a period in a manner which must give a good deal of satisfaction to those in charge. In the cold and wet conditions of that month of January, it is however particularly lacking in attraction for those deputed to it. It is decided to demolish some very dilapidated old huts.

The site is muddy, the old timber wet, filthy, heavy and awkward to handle. When it comes to taking up the floor boards there are rats' nests. Before this is finished, an opportunity occurs for me to take an indoor job in the officers' mess and I take it. Apparently I lack the qualities desirable in a good waiter and there is a nasty accident in which I serve wine from a bottle previously used for paraffin – and back I come into the open air.

However, with the onset of spring, the weather improves and fatigues seem less irksome – particularly to those not too closely supervised – and sometimes it is possible to nip into a cottage for a bowl of coffee without being missed. There are also pleasant orchards behind the farms, where on a Sunday afternoon, one can read or do some letter-writing.

The hamlet of Arqueves, which is our home, is not to be found on any but the largest scale map. When we take our bearings we find that it is in the far north of the Department of the Somme near the border of the Pas de Calais. The nearest town of any size is Doullens and another in the vicinity is Beauval.

We cannot be more than ten miles from the trenches, yet apart from the presence of British troops, signs of war are completely absent. In these days, it is that kind of war. The battle-front has become static. Each side bombards the other's trenches but the long-distance guns are reserved for targets of strategic importance. Bombing from the air has yet to come.

So here we are, within easy range of naval-type guns, with never a qualm – and nothing but an occasional flash in the night sky or a distant boom to remind us of what eventually must await us.

These are the days of the horse. Down at the bottom of the village are our horse-lines. Here are the mounts for the officers, horses to pull the water-cart and the general service wagon, the horse ambulance, and limbers – two-wheeled vehicles, square in shape, for carrying odd impediments when the unit moves.

In fact, we have advanced far enough into the mechanical age to have two or maybe three Talbot motor ambulances. The transport is in the charge of personnel of the Army Service Corps but horse transport and motor transport have no dealings with one another, and though under the direction of our own commanding officer, attend to their own duties with only unofficial contact with the field ambulance men.

However, the cleaning of the vehicles provides one of those useful chores for us and there are times when we are called upon to water and exercise the horses even by means of riding them bareback round a field.

I have mentioned letter-writing and before I complete the picture of this peaceful life in Arqueves in early 1916 and go on *to the next phase, it may be of interest to explain briefly how this is regulated. No letter in an ordinary envelope leaves the unit without being censored locally by one or other of the officers.*

There is, however, a highly prized but rather restricted issue of what are known as "green envelopes", which are sent unopened to base and are censored there. Finally, there is the field postcard, on which by deletion only, one can convey basic information given by the printed lines remaining, such as whether one is well or sick or wounded or due for home leave.

Life is peaceful, though it is boring and frustrating. Contact with other troops is minimal. We are effectively isolated from any sources of news about the progress of the war, most of our activities seem pretty pointless, and any prospect of getting home and resuming civilian life recedes as the weeks go by.

Then there come rumours in the early summer that something is brewing. Towards the end of June these crystallize into whispers of instructions from higher authority reported as having gone through the orderly room, signifying that the days of stagnation will be over shortly. Finally, it is known officially that we are to leave Arqueves for the battle-front for the "Big Push".

At dusk on the last afternoon of the month we parade and start to march. Our spirits are pretty high, partly because any break in our long ordeal of boredom is welcome and partly because, I think, we are more than half sold on the idea that what is about to happen will prove the beginning of the end.

For a few miles we have the road to ourselves. The sky ahead is lit by flashes but still we hear little, for by some freak which can only be due to the conformation of the land, the noise of the bombardment, the greatest ever staged as we afterwards know it to be, reaches us only when we are still nearer the battle-line.

It is when we approach the first small town that we pass through a body of men, presumably infantry, who have fallen out.

Besides those at the sides of the road, we see the glow of cigarettes of others, with some glimpses of vehicles and other equipment half hidden in the trees behind.

As we pass on and having, I think, traversed another village, we come at length to Engelbelmer. My recollection is of an exceptionally wide road with an almost unbroken line of tall blind barn walls on either side.

The noise of artillery has now become a din but suddenly we hear another sound, one we have not heard before, but which we instantly and instinctively recognize as a shell coming our way. Before reaching the ground it bursts, with a noise which drowns all other noise, apparently overhead. I must record with regret that our reactions betray only too clearly that this is our very first experience of being under fire. With one accord, we first duck then break ranks and flatten ourselves against the nearest wall.

The road is left clear for the general service wagon which has been following us. Whether one of the two horses has been touched by some fragment of the shrapnel or has, like us, been thrown into panic by the explosion, the pair bolts taking the wagon and its frantic driver forward on the way we have to go.

We hear afterwards that they are "missing" for some days afterwards, but we, at any rate, re-form and move on without them. Shortly, we halt and in single file turn off into a trench. This becomes deeper as we advance until the parapet is well above our heads and each man's view ahead is limited to the back of the man in front.

Overhead the sky is alive with missiles from our own guns and we see with amazement that we can follow the ascent of some of the thousands of shells as red streaks show along their trajectory.

Our destination proves to be a dug-out, one of the English pattern and very different from the German type with which we later become familiar. It consists of nothing more than a shelter, the floor of which is roughly level with that of the trench and roofed by corrugated iron with layers of sandbags and earth on top.

If the enemy had relied on nothing more resistant to bombardment than this, we should almost certainly have won the coming battle, but they have very different ideas unfortunately for the British infantry. However, there are no falling missiles to disturb us during the night.

5

THE EVE OF THE
BATTLE OF THE SOMME

The extraordinary light-hearted optimism which the preparation for the attack evokes throughout the rank and file is not considered odd in the days leading up to the attack. No serious idea of concealment of the coming onslaught from the enemy is officially entertained. The magnitude of the operation in contemplation makes secrecy impossible, except the precise date.

Nevertheless, it is only by a succession of rumours that the news of what is in store comes to the ordinary serviceman. Hardened as we are to rumours, we know this one is substantial fact. The steadily increasing intensity of the bombardment being carried out by our artillery, the special training and special equipment introduced in our own unit and every other with which we come into contact, coupled with the universal feeling of expectancy, leads us to the belief that we are in for something bigger than has been seen ever before.

We see in it a definite prospect of a victorious end to the war. The first result we visualize is the finish of trench warfare. After that, there might be hard work but it will be, so we think, in the nature of rapid trekking after a fleeing enemy. In the spirit of elation in which we live throughout the month of June 1916, our minds become impressionable to every detail with which life just then is filled.

The simple details of the French village in which we are billeted, the barns in which we sleep, the establishments where summer thirst is quenched, the houses where we are regaled with egg and chips; these and every detail imprint themselves so effectually on the memory that they remain, in spite of all the more stirring later experiences, as part of the recollections associated with 1 July.

In my mind there is nothing clearer in the memory than the sounds of the gramophone which plays interminably before the window of the Sergeants' Mess and the banal melodies which are all its poor repertoire of records can offer.

The climax of this fever of anticipation comes on the evening of 30 June. Marching orders finally set the seal of truth on rumour. Shortly before sunset, we are mustered for parade for what we have no doubt is the last time in that little village street we know so well.

We set forth with ambulances and everyone in train, perhaps a little awed by the proximity of the great event before us, but with greater and more solid enthusiasm than ever moved us before or after.

As the daylight fades we see the flashes of the guns but as yet hear nothing but our own movements and conversation. After an hour or so of marching, we halt where the road is extra dark from the shadow of a wood. Here comes the first evidence that others are bound in the same direction. Among the trees apparently are horses and limbers, men mounted and on foot – the champing of bits, stamping of hoofs, the calling of orders – and the lights of glowing cigarettes among the shadowy forms.

Presently we move on and find ourselves once more alone. On we march through a village well known to us, now quiet and peaceful, the civilian inhabitants abed. We move on further till at length we reach another hamlet, where war is evidently closer at hand. Roofs and walls bear signs of occasional shells. Sandbag protections tell of unpleasant possibilities and suddenly we get our baptism of fire.

The noise of the bombardment is now fairly audible but a different sound strikes our nervous ears, similar to the approach of an express train which as yet is new to us, but which we know for what it is. A shell bursts fairly close to our column. A roof nearby apparently finishes its period of usefulness.

Shards of red hot metal and other solid matter fall about us and we start to seek cover where there is none. One pair of horses bolts with a wagon and are seen no more by us. It is we who remain unwillingly. Only a few of us have "tin hats" and the less fortunate of us without one soon become all too painfully conscious of the inadequacy of soft caps.

This night, however, we encounter no more perils. Soon we come to the trenches, very neat and comforting in their protectiveness. We march in single file on duckboards, round traverses and past fire-steps. Now we are in the thick of the den of battle with a vengeance.

All around us we are aware of the presence of batteries of our own guns and we hear the onslaught of the ear-splitting discharge of shells and from the gunners the nerve-shattering voices at close quarters as they load them. This is the first time for most of us. We are virgin soldiers.

Someone observes that in the darkness of the sky the track of the shells is visible in faint red streaks. We marvel that they cross and re-cross without occasional collision.

At last we halt and here we stay the night.

Whether we sleep that night I do not remember. Certainly there is no memory of sleeplessness – and some men, I do recall, snore loudly. Perhaps the night is unconsciously wiped from the recollection by the traumatic impressions of the succeeding day.

All that matters anyhow is that we have taken our place to act whatever part might be allocated to us in the great battle. For my part I lie in a trench open to the night. I recall reflecting on how I came to be there.

6

THE FIRST DAY OF
THE SOMME

Prologue

The Battle of the Somme was the long-planned major 1916 offensive against the Germans. Largely a British and Empire effort, it was designed to relieve some of the pressure on the French who were being severely tested by the Germans at Verdun. It was also the first experience of a large-scale offensive for many of the New Army units in France, including many of the "Pals Battalions" that had been formed when men from a specific local area joined up together en masse. It was also the introduction to serious fighting with heavy casualties for Charles Horton's field ambulance unit.

The coming Somme offensive was known as "The Big Push" (a term Charles Horton himself uses) and the British went into it with some confidence. A week-long artillery barrage, of such intensity that it is said to have been heard across the channel in Kent, was expected to wipe out the German barbed wire, trench systems, defences and most of the defenders themselves. The assault troops were expected to walk – not run – across no-man's-land, bearing heavy packs weighing about 70 pounds, and occupy the opposing trenches without difficulty.

Of course, that first day on the Somme, 1 July 1916, became notoriously the bloodiest day in the history of the British Army; there were 57,470 casualties, of whom 19,240 were killed or died from their wounds. For many, including the members of Horton's field ambulance unit, the first day of the battle, which went on to last four-and-a-half months, encapsulated the war's futility and sacrifice. The first day on the Somme has always overshadowed the many days that followed, even though they also saw a scarcely imaginable human cost for both sides.

Certainly, the first day provided an impossible task for the stretcher bearers. The well-built German defences were not obliterated, the barbed wire still presented a considerable barrier, and many of the defending troops had survived in dugouts deep underground. When the artillery barrage ceased the German front-line troops knew the attack was imminent. They emerged to man the defences, including the machine-guns, that took so many lives.

The New Army units were raw and could not have received any training that would have prepared them for the maelstrom they entered on 1 July. It would have been unfair to expect great demonstrations of tactical acumen or initiative from troops who had only been in uniform a short time and who had limited combat experience. This was not the regular Army of 1914; the British Expeditionary Force was long gone.

At various points along the line of the attack, notably on the right – the French flank – the first day objectives were taken, and in some cases held. Some local commanders took their troops into no-man's-land early, under cover of darkness, so that they could storm the opposing trenches as soon as the barrage lifted; for example, the 1st Lancashire Fusiliers assembled overnight in a sunken road in the middle of no-man's-land. In most cases, these initiatives were no more successful than the British assault elsewhere.

The day was long in early July, but when darkness finally began to fall those wounded who were able began to crawl back towards the British lines. The stretcher bearers, of course, were active throughout the first day of the Somme. There were instances of German troops respecting the work of stretcher bearers and medical teams, but much of the time anyone showing themselves in no-man's-land was liable to be fired upon.

Sunday 1 July is a beautiful summer's day, but the sun is still low in the sky when many thousands of young men feel its rays for the last time. The assault troops are to go over the top at 7.30 a.m.

It is some time after midday when we ambulance men witness for ourselves at close quarters, the first evidence of the disaster which has befallen the attackers. We emerge from the trench system at a point named Knightsbridge. We notice that the trenches we have seen that day are all named after famous London thoroughfares – the idea, no doubt, of London troops who inhabit them. The other names have faded from memory, but that one name will always mean to me that spot in France.

It is an open space which had once been a peaceful field. It is now a collecting place for stretcher cases, line upon line of them on the ground in the hot sun with flies settling on bloodstained bandages, some quite still, others able to raise a head for a cigarette or a drink of water or tea.

Padres here and there are bending down to talk to the wounded and one, a Roman Catholic priest, administers the last sacrament. Just within sight are trucks on a light railway which we understand leads to the casualty clearing station.

The stretchers wait their turn to be loaded four on a truck. There is only mechanical traction. I do not remember seeing a horse. We newcomers give a hand in supplying drinks and in stretcher-carrying, but there are many still to be moved when we are called upon to form up with, at last, apparently some definite duties to perform.

We are led back into the trenches by our commanding officer, accompanied by a guide and a regimental medical officer, and the news filters through that we are to pick up stretchers from a store and then proceed in the direction of the front line. The hours of daylight have passed and presently we halt in darkness and learn that we have taken the wrong route.

Soon after, we about-turn and we run into sudden trouble. There is a stunning explosion above us and I feel bits of earth falling on the steel helmet I have acquired, as have other members of our party, to replace the cloth caps we started with. Immediately in front of me – and not two paces away – a man who has come from England with me falls forward on his face and moans quietly once. He is the one who found me in the park near my home on the day I volunteered and a good friend. He is dead when he is picked up. Eight or ten paces ahead, the commanding officer is another casualty, with a thigh wound which takes him eventually to "Blighty".

Just around the traverse behind me, a corporal cook has a severe foot injury. We who survive proceed under the command of the regimental medical officer. We find out that we have been seconded from the South Midland Division, to which we are normally attached, to the 29th Division, recently moved from the Dardanelles and made up to strength again after their shattering losses.

We move into a trench with fire-steps and on one of these is the cold figure of a boy of not more than 18, killed apparently before he ever left the trench that morning, and possibly like ourselves, in the trenches for the first time.

In a few moments we are climbing out of the trench into no-man's-land. We pass through our own barbed wire and upon this at intervals see bodies of men who have died before finding the way through. Under an order quite unfamiliar to us RAMC men, but which we take to mean that each man is to halt at so many paces from the one in front, we start our work of finding any bodies which still have life in them and carrying them back.

There is no lack of light as "Verey" flares, from one side or the other, burst and hang in the sky then drop. We busy ourselves at our task, and in the thrill of being able to rescue first one and then another and another for whom there is still hope, the craven fears which at first assail us, almost cease to bother us.

There is no sign of any hostility from the enemy trenches and that, too, reassures us so that when there are no more stretchers and three of us find ourselves left behind in no-man's-land, we do the only thing we can for those who still live within our limited area of search, which is to carry them to our own trench.

In the hope that more stretcher bearers will soon appear, we lower our patients as carefully as we can and lay them at the bottom of the trench and wait. Nobody comes. We are evidently in a forward trench not normally manned or patrolled. We do what we can for the poor chaps on the ground, though we have no dressings, no food, and no water, except the little in our own bottles and one we find. Two are in agony from wounds in leg joints and none can bear for us to move them.

We debate whether to split up and for two of us to go in search of help, but such explorations as we make give no glimmer or indication of which way to go and on the whole we can see no alternative to staying put.

It is after a very long night has given way to day that our solitude ends. We are able to hand over our charges and are conducted to our unit to explain what has happened, to learn that we have been posted as "missing". We receive much-needed refreshment.

The services of the ambulance are not further called upon in that "Beaumont Hamel-Serre Sector" and it is next day, 3 July, that we leave it. Before we march, however, there is a heavy thunderstorm, with torrential rain, which floats the duckboards laid across the sumps in the trenches.

Also a "fatigue" is found for us, which consists in recovering from the ground above our dug-out all the sound tins of bully-beef which the watchful eye of the officer-in-charge notices lying discarded by some former tenants of our resting-place. It sticks in the memory as a resounding anti-climax to the "baptism of fire" which we have survived.

Bert Horton in RAMC uniform

7

THE BATTLE OF
THE SOMME

We sleep at the end of our march under bivouacs improvised from our groundsheets in a field at the village of Bus-en-Artois. Next morning, having dismantled the bivouacs, tidied ourselves up, and breakfasted, we parade under our new CO who feels moved to address us in complimentary terms on the way we have come through our recent ordeal.

He then hands us over to the sergeant major who has not accompanied us on our trip, from whom we have a further and very contrasting speech. He begins by referring to the CO's words of praise and says that he is now going to "give it to us in the bleeding neck".

What, and whose, is the crime, we wonder, which so arouses his ire? We are all, it shortly transpires, in dire disgrace for having left a quantity of litter visible after striking our nocturnal shelters. He proceeds, as usual, to "fall out the sanitary men", but the responsibility for finding and removing the offensive litter is laid upon all who have no special duties.

Later we march off to fresh billets and my recollection is that we stay in several different villages in the course of the next two or three weeks. When we go into the line again, it is at a point some distance southwards of Beaumont Hamel, perhaps a dozen miles, and our last march takes us through Albert. We look up at the famous Golden Virgin, a statue once standing erect on the steeple of the church, but at this time hanging horizontally, held from complete collapse only by the steel bars concealed in the figure.

The town is very near to the original line of battle and has suffered considerably from gunfire, but now we are to find that British attacks following the initial onslaught of 1 July have succeeded to the extent of pushing the line back a mile or two – and Albert at that moment is quiet.

Pressing on, we come to Crucifix Corner, a road junction which was once marked by one of the wayside shrines – not uncommon in the French countryside – but which is now no longer visible. We halt and fall out to be divided into small groups, each of two or three stretcher parties of four. My group is told that we are bound for Ovillers. We are to relieve men from another section of the ambulance who have already done a spell at the post in question. While waiting for our guide, we climb a bank from which it is possible to see the spot, about a mile away, for which we are destined.

For the first time we gaze upon what is to be known as the devastated area. Few people now living can have any conception of what the fair countryside of France suffered as this ever-widening swathe of desolation swept down from Belgium south-westwards. From our vantage point, we look upon a man-made desert stretching to the horizon on which we can distinguish no landmarks but clumps of what were once trees clustered round little hamlets, but now lifeless sticks, bereft of branches, with no sign of any human habitation remaining above ground.

Over one such clump of trees there appears as we watch a dark blotch of smoke – exploding shrapnel. That, we are told is Ovillers. We first march or, rather, walk, as there is no longer *any formality in our progress, along a road which has obviously been reconstructed with local materials, rutted with wheels of military vehicles.*

In a shallow valley on our right are many 18-pounder batteries discharging shells from time to time with noisy reports and puffs of smoke and flame. Shell-holes and old trenches are distinguishable by the chalk of upturned subsoil and ahead we see more puffs of smoke in the summer sky.

At length, we turn left into a shallow trench and at once become aware of that horrible stench, compounded of rotting human flesh and chloride of lime, which is to be in our nostrils night and day so long as we serve at the Ovillers post.

As we negotiate repeated traverses, the trench grows deeper but often we are able to see over the uneven parapet and always there are bodies in German uniforms strewing the ground. Bodies have been used to build the parapet and in places they lie not completely covered by earth under our feet. These had been German trenches and our post is a German dug-out, the first we have seen.

The entrance is, I suppose, about four feet high and now that it has changed hands, naturally faces the wrong way. All the same, when one has descended the six or eight steps to the floor below and finds one can stand upright and walk about in a chamber 10 or 12 feet square, one feels a considerable sense of security, a comforting prospect, at least, for our off-duty spells.

We find, however, that we are "on call" for all 24 hours of the day, that most of our calls come at night and that we seldom have as much as a two-hour break during the hours of darkness – enough to swallow a mug of tea and perhaps to drop off to sleep before being awakened by the call of "next squad out". It is a daunting call when it comes at two or three in the morning. Reluctantly casting off the blanket, swallowing another drink of tea… one climbs the steps of the dug-out shivering in the night air and mentally cringing at the sounds of guns and shells and at the prospect ahead of us.

Carrying a folded stretcher we turn left toward the front line, the condition of the trench worsening as we plod on around the traverses. Seldom do we meet or have to pass any other men until we approach the regimental aid post. There we come across infantry in small groups around the entrances of what dug-outs are still tenantable.

I well remember one which is not. Some fairly recent shell-burst has filled the entrance until only a crack is visible under the wooden crossbeam over the stairway, and through that crack protrude the fingers of two lifeless hands.

Having been led to our patient we lay him on our stretcher with a blanket over him and start our journey back. Carrying in trenches we naturally have to take turns, with one man at each end of the stretcher and the remaining two disposed in front and rear ready to help lifting it, when necessary, head high to negotiate difficult corners.

Slings over the shoulders help to relieve the pull on the hands and wrists but still it is hard work and we change places from time to time. We pass our own post and press on toward the road, feeling with our feet what have become familiar "landmarks". One is a discarded bag of Mills bombs with one grenade showing above ground and already polished with the passing of feet; then the rump of a buried body, which gives a little to the heavy pressure of a boot. Once we are out on the road it is possible to discard the slings and make speedier and easier progress with one man at each corner of the stretcher, bearing it on one hand or on his shoulder.

So we deliver our charge at the dressing station, to be examined and treated in the bright light of acetylene lamps – the smell of which, combined with the fumes of iodine and other chemical and human odours, remains a lasting memory.

Another swig of tea and back to our post at Ovillers, possibly to get some sleep, possibly not, if there is another summons to be obeyed and the other squad not yet returned. Our physique at this time is tough and resilient, but as night succeeds night, one senses the cumulative effect of these conditions on nerves and morale. So when there is the chance to take a night off, I take it with relief.

The dug-out in which I am offered the prospect of a few hours uninterrupted slumber is of the British type, one of a number set in a low bank near Crucifix Corner, noisy from the banging of surrounding light artillery and protected on top with the usual corrugated iron and sandbags.

When one has crawled in, one finds about as much cubic space as under a kitchen table. The sides and earth floor are covered in hessian and the front door is a blanket. There is already one occupant asleep and I lie covering myself with a blanket in the unoccupied area. I do not sleep for long. I detect the smell of singeing and some unaccustomed warmth around my feet which rouses me. My bedfellow has gone, but on his departure has evidently left a lighted candle which has burned down until it has ignited the hessian, now smouldering in a widening hole in all directions. I deal with this and having satisfied myself that the fire is out, I let in some fresh air to clear the smoke. I settle down once more.

It is still not daylight when the voice of an NCO calls upon me to emerge as there is a job to be done. A new draft has been sent out to the ambulance from England and I am introduced to four of them and told of the expedition ahead of us. Under my guidance we are to collect a case from a section of the line to the left of Ovillers known as Blighty Wood. We have heard it spoken of in terms of loathing and awe as being several degrees less comfortable than Ovillers and here am I on what is to have been my night off, acting as leader, being the only seasoned member of the first party from the ambulance to test the truth of this estimate.

Soon we are in very deep and undamaged trenches and from the pitch darkness the "wood" must still have some foliage. One of the recruits, all of whom seem to be in good heart, hits upon the resourceful idea of attaching his luminous wrist-watch to the back of his tin hat for the benefit of the man behind.

Inevitably we soon emerge into an area of general and recent devastation illuminated with Verey lights, the ground beneath our feet broken and uneven. Artillery is active and we duck apprehensively as one shell seems to burst very near.

A little further on we find that this, or some other near-miss, has blocked the trench with a four-foot pile of earth over which we clamber, and presently we are at the end of our outward journey. Our burden is an unconscious German prisoner and we find, alas, when we deliver him at the aid post, that our toil and sweat has been devoted for some time to a lifeless body.

We are soon withdrawn from Ovillers and when we see that unsavoury spot again, it is from the other side of the valley at La Boisselle, another obliterated village on the road to Bapaume and famous in its day for the gigantic crater lying just below it. The story of its origin is that both sides are tunnelling at this spot to lay charges prior to attack. The detonation of one lot of explosives sets off the other and the result is a hole many feet deep to the rim and yards in circumference.

From La Boisselle, a branch road leads right to Contalmaison where the ambulance later makes its headquarters in a chateau standing on an eminence overlooking another crossroads and remaining intact in its lower storey.

From here squads are sent in turn to serve in forward posts but for a time I have the good fortune to act as orderly on one of the motor ambulances journeying from time to time to the casualty clearing station beyond Albert, as well as running odd errands for the officers' mess.

In what is on the whole a most welcome spell from more arduous and perilous duties, two incidents remain in the memory. One is a punctured tyre one night in Albert when an odd shell or two of shrapnel bursting overhead leads to what must be one of the quickest wheel-changes ever performed away from Brooklands racing-track. The other is a dense fog on the road home from La Boisselle when I have to walk in front of the vehicle bearing a white handkerchief to safeguard the driver from the deep and quite unprotected ditches at each side of the road.

My turn comes to serve at Martinpuich, a forward post in territory vacated by the enemy only in the previous few weeks. The country between Contalmaison and Martinpuich is gently undulating. Taking the direct route across what is devastated land we come to a downward slope on which a light railway line has been used for military purposes, the vehicles being little trucks drawn by ponies. Now all are dead, the rails broken and twisted by shell-fire, trucks lying overturned, and every few yards the swelling bodies of the traction animals.

This is the first evidence we have seen of animal casualties, for while no doubt horses are largely used by artillery and for transport of supplies, their work does not usually bring them far into the forward areas where bombardment is most intense. This line, however, must have been operated under enemy observation in desperate disregard of massive attack from enemy artillery. Hell must have raged here for man and beast, but all traces of human losses are removed, and only the dead ponies are left lying to rot. There is something especially repellent in the sight of this animal sacrifice.

It is at Martinpuich – or the approach to it – that we become acquainted with that phenomenon which has come to be regarded as the speciality of the Flanders wartime scene – or one of them, the other being the ubiquitous, cheerful corn poppy. What we now encounter is mud!

Down in the little valley before Martinpuich, there may well have been in better times an innocent stream taking surplus water harmlessly away. Now there is a small lake of churned-up earth and water of the consistency of thin porridge. For the moment, however, we are able to avoid this by taking a duckboard track on which we complete our journey to the German dug-out which is our post.

This is by far the deepest we have seen – 15 or 20 steps down, but I remember little more of it since duty soon calls me elsewhere. The squad in which I am one of four is directed to a position at the side of the road which leads up from the lake of mud.

On this trip, there is no way but through it. As no gum-boots are available, we are thoughtfully advised to wrap sandbags around our puttees. We pass to comparatively dry ground with several layers of assorted textile material acting as filter, but this does not entirely impede the passage of moisture to our ankles and calves and down into our boots. We never discover the precise purpose of our mission, but it involves taking possession of what is no more than a covered hole at the side of the road and big enough to take two lying down or four squatting.

The chief point of interest in an otherwise featureless and apparently uninhabited landscape is one of the original, enormously heavy tanks, standing idly almost in front of the entrance to our post, the first of these new weapons of war that we have seen at close quarters. As the road is cut into sloping ground, the bank on the enemy side is just high enough to conceal the monster from direct observation, but it does occur to us that, should its presence become known, it will be much safer inside its armoured walls than in our highly inadequate dug-out.

However, our stint of 48 hours or so in this spot passes entirely without incident, as does, as far as I can recall, the rest of our spell in Martinpuich. The destruction of this village, we find, has not been as complete as at Ovillers.

We deem conditions are quiet enough to permit a little exploration of one or two cottages where the foundations and parts of the walls remain. A few discarded letters and postcards, the only rewards for our curiosity, serve to remind us that this man-made desert – now our familiar environment – was, but a few months before, inhabited by people to whom the village postman brought messages from friends and relatives. Where are they now, these innocent folk whose lives have been so rudely and tragically disrupted by this senseless war?

By Christmas 1916 we complete six months of spells on various sections of the Somme Front. We are lucky enough to spend the festivities out of the line and celebrate with a dinner of roast pork, plum pudding, and drinks served on a table with plates and civilized cutlery.

This alternates with a vast amount of marching from one rest billet to another and periods when we run sick hospitals. On these occasions, when we assume the role of orderly in small wards, which are either huts or marquees, our patients seldom suffer from anything more serious or prolonged than what we now call "flu". Then it is designated "PUO", meaning "Pyrexia [fever] of unknown origin".

In France we somehow escape the type of influenza which, as we learn afterwards, so seriously ravages the population at home. Our cases respond very predictably to the tablets of phenacetin – since ousted by aspirin – supplemented by "dover's powder"[5] or the standard pills known by numbers in the RAMC stock of remedies – number nines for constipation – as necessary.

Our officers, of course, now revert to their character of medical practitioners, receiving our reports on temperature, pulse, and respiration for each patient in turn, making any examinations considered necessary, and finally prescribing further treatment, of which we take notes using with no little pride and a touch of professionalism the medical shorthand we have acquired, such as "t.d.s." and "p.c.".

The new year 1917 brings a severe and prolonged frost, and our attire becomes much more picturesque with the issue of leather or goatskin jerkins with the fur outside. We have the good fortune to be out of the line during this period but find ourselves first in the vicinity of Becourt and Fricourt – still within ten miles of Albert in a south-westerly direction – an area of utter desolation since it has been the scene of some of the bloodiest fighting in the Somme offensive. This, however, was some months earlier and the line here has been pushed forward to a safe distance.

It is here that I have to have treatment for an attack of impetigo, a rather repulsive, scabby skin complaint, the all too common consequence of contact with infected blankets. I remember it causes me to be removed from one of my most congenial jobs, serving tea in a canteen we set up for patients and other odd callers needing revival in the bitterly cold conditions prevailing.

I recover sufficiently by the time the main body of the ambulance moves on, to be left behind on a "rear party" charged with the demolition and removal of a tent hospital left standing apparently by another ambulance which has preceded ours.

There are I suppose, some 20 or 30 bell-tents to be struck, rolled into bundles, taken down a slope to a railway siding, and there loaded into waiting trucks. We few left behind have as our billet a Nissen hut with a Canadian stove and we enjoy for a few days a carefree existence working hard in the hours of daylight, but resting, eating, and sleeping comfortably – albeit on bare boards – and absolved, due to a shortage of water, from any undue observance of strict rules as to washing and shaving.

The complication in our assignment lies in the fact that the bell-tents are frozen in a wet condition and the tent pegs are immovably fixed in iron-hard ground. So, with the approval of the corporal in charge of the operation, we hack through the guy ropes with axes, leave the pegs where they are and by brute force bend, rather than fold, the canvas into something in the nature of a bundle. Eventually we clear the encampment and load it as directed.

We rejoin our unit at a little town called Cappy, boasting among other urban features, shops and a two-storey school in which we are billeted. Below the school playground is a canal, now frozen like all the meres and lakes which we are to discover in the neighbouring district.

Here we drop into the routine of parades and fatigues, but I remember a considerable amount of free time in which we behave like schoolboys on the ice. In the absence of skates, which naturally are not available, we make huge slides, on which our nail-studded army boots rest adequately.

The presence of some French troops among us illustrates a curious difference in our national attitudes to the queue system. We all slid in a long line in one direction and walk back to the starting point – which seems the natural thing to do. Our French friends think otherwise and risk collision by sliding back instead of walking.

Our beds are on the upper floor and they are, of course, on the floor, lit in the daytime by skylights in the sloping roof. One evening as we lie, or sit reading, or otherwise filling in the early hours of darkness, we are startled to see above us a reddish glow through the skylights with sparks falling on the glass.

It seemed almost certain that our own building is on fire and we each gather into our haversacks our most treasured private possessions and go downstairs. Once outside we see that the fire is on the other side of the canal in a very large wooden building occupied by infantry.

A few people bent on making a gesture of help have hacked a hole in the ice and we see an odd canvas bucket or two filled with water and carried away but there are no fire engines and no evidence at all from our viewpoint of any more likely efforts being made to combat the flames. Already it is obvious that no such efforts could have made any difference. The rattle of exploding cartridges testify to burning equipment, the luminous cracks in the planking of the walls widen and brighten into flames as the whole structure becomes ignited and burns like a prepared bonfire.

We soon decide that the best of the spectacle is over and retire to our billet wondering how it has started and what would happen to the person or persons found to be responsible. We hear later that retribution falls upon the whole company concerned – in the form of stoppage of leave.

Winter has given way to spring when we make our next move and march into Peronne. On this sector the enemy has made a planned retirement of a dozen miles or more and the city of Peronne, which until recently has been far enough behind the German line to escape anything more than superficial damage, is now once more a relatively safe place in its new occupation.

It has, however, been thoroughly sacked and, as we are warned, planted with booby traps. Nevertheless, the school premises that we take over for a sick-hospital and billets are quite well preserved and, when we solve the heating problem by scrounging stoves from derelict houses, it is quite comfortable.

We receive as patients only the sick among our own men and neighbouring troops and being appointed to night duty, I find it possible to snatch sufficient rest. This avoids me having to waste daylight hours, which would in any case be unprofitable with day-duty men using the same sleeping quarters. So there is opportunity for exploration of the neighbourhood and primitive aquatic sport on improvised rafts in the surrounding stretches of shallow water.

Life in Peronne, while it seems when we think of it, to be lacking in much useful purpose, is as easy and pleasant as any we have experienced in our months of active service. When we march out – past the blossoming but decapitated fruit trees left behind by the retreating enemy, it is the start of a series of moves which take us northwards again through some of the old battlefields to Bapaume and on a few miles to a spot called Beugny.

The flattish plain which surrounds us here is almost unscathed and the distant rising ground where we understand the battle-line now runs, presents the normal tree-covered aspect of this part of northern France. We spend here some uneventful weeks, living in huts, running a sick-hospital and engaging in yet another new type of "fatigue".

A mile or two northwards along the Bapaume–Cambrai highway, a sunken road branches to the left, and at a spot where the bank is highest we are set, a small party at a time, to the construction of a dug-out. The job involves digging first downward for a yard or two and then tunnelling horizontally, the material being soft red sandstone.

We never find out who has initiated this enterprise or whether any expert mind has directed the location or the precise method of tackling the excavation and reinforcing it against collapse. However, we strip to the waist in the fine, warm weather. We cheerfully dig with picks and shovels and wedge the timbering in, in what somebody in authority prescribes as the right manner. We never finish it and it is doubtful whether, if ever completed, it is put to use but we hear later that when the Engineers see what we have done they are surprised we have not buried ourselves. In their view, the timbering would have collapsed if a shell had fallen within 50 yards of it.

From our headquarters at Beugny, we go no nearer the line than to man a post a mile or so forward at the side of another by-road running over some rising ground. This has no banks to hide it from observation and we are told not to show ourselves in daylight but to keep in the cover of a dug-out – British type – which we also use for sleeping.

However, neither do we see nor do we hear any indication of enemy interest in this lonely spot and the object of the enterprise is not readily apparent. We are, as it turns out, not to see anything more of the fighting in France or to do any more stretcher-bearing on this front and in a short time entrain for some more northerly part of the line, which turns out to be the Ypres Salient.

8

THE THIRD BATTLE OF YPRES (PASSCHENDAELE)

PROLOGUE

The Third Battle of Ypres ran from late July until November 1917. It was a major offensive with ambitions to break out of the Ypres Salient and push the Germans back to the Belgian coast, but it quickly became another major battle of attrition, with small gains made at the cost of appalling casualties on both sides. It is commonly now known as the Battle of Passchendaele, taking the name of an obliterated village captured by Canadian troops shortly before the close of the offensive.

Flanders is flat, low-lying country and the "ridges" towards which the British advanced are barely discernible; this landscape, and an unusually high summer rainfall, created the wet, muddy conditions for which the battle is now infamous. Wounded men drowned in the mud, it immobilized transport, and stretcher bearers struggled to bring casualties back through the morass. Often, eight bearers would be required for a single casualty owing to the muddy conditions, the weight of the mud-plastered stretcher, and the soaked clothing of the wounded man. The battlefield became a shattered wasteland because of the shellfire, which also took a heavy toll of stretcher bearers.

After the capture of Passchendaele, the battle fizzled out; both sides were left exhausted. The Germans had suffered around 250,000 casualties, the British, Canadians and Australians around 300,000. Today, the Tyne Cot Memorial Cemetery situated close to the scene of the final stages of the Passchendaele attrition, is the largest Commonwealth War Graves Commission cemetery in the world. Tens of thousands of the Commonwealth soldiers remembered here have no known grave, their remains perhaps atomised during bombardments or lost in the mud of the battlefield. It is a sombre place and captures the feeling that the very word "Passchendaele" now conjures up, one of waste and futility. Certainly, the battle affected Bert Horton very strongly for the rest of his life.

> *...I died in Hell*
> *(They called it Passchendaele.) My wound was slight*
> *And I was hobbling back; and then a shell*
> *Burst slick upon the duckboards: so I fell*
> *into the bottomless mud, and lost the light.*
> **Siegfried Sassoon**

I remember little of the train journey, except that it is a Sunday evening, a normal and peaceful Sunday evening apparently in the townships through which we pass, though our route runs roughly parallel to the battle-line at a distance which nowhere is more than 30 miles.

Yet we see civilians, which have become a rare sight to us, enjoying the evening sunshine, some of them in their back garden. This is the first time ever that we have been privileged to move from Place A to Place B without being called upon to march the distance with our luggage on our backs.

While enjoying the experience I think we feel a presentiment that the object is not to save our flat feet but to save time in getting us into position for more serious work than we have had to perform in recent months. We are never far away from the rest of the division, so the infantry must have moved or be moving too, and not for rest or recreation. I do not suppose I am the only traveller on that train whose thoughts turn to what our own folk at home are doing on that pleasant Sunday evening.

We detrain somewhere near Poperinghe, just over the French border in that tiny corner of Belgium, which still remains, at terrible cost, in Allied occupation. We arrive after a short march at what is to be the ambulance headquarters for some months.

It is a little collection of army huts, which we come to know as Gwent Farm. Adjoining the huts are the horse-lines; everything is neat and tidy and the whole unit is once more assembled more closely than it has been for many months.

All is peaceful, except for the occasional noise of distant gunfire and the nightly whine of long-range shells sailing over us towards Poperinghe, aimed, we understand at the labour camps in front of the town.

Fatigues are so inadequate to occupy us that at times we are taken on short route marches, which without packs are in the nature of pleasant walks. A party of us is returning from one of these and has entered the entrance road through the horse-lines when with awesome suddenness there is the sound of a shell coming apparently right on top of us – and the explosion follows in a split second.

As we straighten up we know that it has fallen not on the road but in the horse-lines and not 20 yards away. It leaves no crater, being evidently of the type that bursts upon impact, but has obviously fallen within a few feet of a portable forge.

A young driver, who was standing at the forge boiling up some water for a drink of tea, is now lying with a fearful wound in the head and obviously beyond help. He had been a clerk in the office of Birmingham University and had once been the one to take my father's cheque for my term fee.

Nearby is a corporal returned only the previous day from leave in the course of which he has married. There is widespread devastation too among the horses. Several are lying dead and others standing with a strange absence of panic or indeed any obvious sign of pain, with all too evident wounds. When a quick survey of the damage to the animals is made, it is the distasteful task of our CO to use the revolver with which he alone is provided to shoot nearly a dozen. Thus we learn of the special hazards of living in a salient, vulnerable from all directions to gunfire of almost any range.

We continue to sleep in the huts with as much fatalism as we can command, but worried at times by the attention of one battery which appears to be firing at regularly increasing range, with shell bursts getting nearer and louder until they pass beyond us and we feel we can relax.

I recall not more than two weeks elapse before the time comes for us to move forward for active duty. The sequence of events in this sector is much less clear for some reason than those I can recount in more or less chronological order as happening on the Somme.

I have my ten days' leave from Gwent Farm in September 1917 after 20 months overseas service and come back there for more work in front of Ypres, so that puts our stay in this area at not less than three months.

As we first approach the battle area on the north side of Ypres and face the same desert of devastation as we have seen on the Somme, the obvious difference is the lack of trenches. In place of dug-outs are concrete erections above ground called "pillboxes". These are connected by "duckboards" – parallel sawn timbers of about four feet by two with strips laid across – on which troops move in single file. As far as possible, we keep to the road. It affords no protection but neither do the duckboards and when a loaded stretcher has to be carried, it enables all four bearers to take a corner each, so halving the weight and speeding the rate of progress.

Again, we work night and day, whenever the call comes for "next squad out", so that sleep is irregular and sometimes scanty. So far as we can judge, all the attacking is done by our own troops and our own artillery. There are no large-scale assaults in our time like we have seen on the Somme, but nightly infantry raids with supporting bombardment.

We have no means of knowing what harm these do to the Germans, but the steady stream of casualties with which we have to deal is evidence enough of the cost on our side. We are busiest of course at night time and frequently we pick our way with laden stretcher round shell-holes and assorted obstructions in the dark with only a vague sense of direction, but ultimately gaining the road which leads us to our destination, the dressing station.

These cross-country treks, which seem to engender a sort of protective fatalism in us, always appears to be in complete isolation from any company but our own. It is only when a salvo from one of our own batteries unexpectedly makes an ear-shattering addition to the noises of the night that we realize that others beside ourselves have duties in the vicinity. I never remember meeting a soul from whom we might ask the way or get a cheery greeting.

It is in the midday sunshine that the incident occurs that perhaps remains clearest in the memory. My squad is following in the wake of another, some 50 yards ahead on this selfsame road, each party with a loaded stretcher carried shoulder-high, when with a swish and a very loud report a shell explodes ahead of us and the squad in front collapses to the ground.

We hurry forward and find that only one of the bearers has suffered actual injury and he is prostrate with a horrible gash in the flesh of his thigh. Each of us carries what is called a "shell-dressing", consisting of a large pad of cotton wool covered in gauze with an ampoule of iodine, the whole wrapped in an oilskin pouch and we apply one of these and bandage it on, the first time, strangely enough, that we give such first aid.

I have met my wounded comrade many times since, minus a leg and he is able to set at rest the nagging doubt I feel for a long time that some fault of mine in the first treatment of his injury had been the factor which led to amputation.

Another particular incident stays in my mind. My section of the ambulance has had a long and wearing spell of forward duty and rejoices at last in the news that we are being moved back from our post with the prospect, as we think, of a spell of rest.

We spend the night in another and larger "pillbox" where we lie down where we can find space. I am unlucky in finding nothing better than a sort of ledge or the top of a cupboard, not more than a foot wide, the only place available. On this I lie quite sleepless, not only because of the discomfort of my couch, but the distraction of hearing the periodic pumping of a primus stove, on which a "dixie" of porridge is being prepared for our breakfast.

Presently there comes also the sound of shuffling feet on the duckboard outside as a party of infantrymen move in single file in the darkness in the direction from which we have come. After our porridge and a drink of tea, we follow them. It is just another night attack and our job is to bring back the unfortunate ones who are, though still alive, not able to walk back.

We cannot determine the purpose of our marching rearwards a mile or so and thus having that much further to walk up to battalion headquarters from which we start our stretcher-bearing. On arrival at battalion HQ in early daylight, we have time to look around. Forward, the ground rises gently toward the Passchendaele Ridge from which the enemy look down on the Ypres Salient.

In the shallow valley running left and right, the ground is churned and sterile and one or two Royal Engineers (Signals) are looking for breaks in the wires running along the surface. One of them turns round to look at us RAMC men and I recognize him as a boy who was in the same Sunday School class as myself five or six years before. I have not spoken to him since, but have once seen him driving a horse-drawn milk float. We greet each other and chat for a few moments until he returns to his perilous job and I wander towards the pillbox where we have to wait. Inside, the officers are evidently being served with breakfast, for we are confronted with the tantalizing smell of frying bacon.

However, it is mixed with another smell, the one with which we have lived in Ovillers; the stink of putrefying flesh. It comes from the bodies of German soldiers lying in a pile at one side of the concrete stronghold, having perhaps died in the effort to defend it.

Back at Gwent Farm, for our periodic rests we are able to make a number of visits to Poperinghe, a substantial town by our standards, still having a civilian population and showing little damage, though as I have said, within the range of gunfire.

I blow the organ in the church to enable one of our men, who is a practised organist, to test its condition. I visit, of course, the since-famous Talbot House, better known as Toc H, where tea and slab cake are dispensed at reasonable prices on the ground floor and spiritual refreshment at the hands of the Reverend "Tubby" Clayton, in a room upstairs.

There is also a pleasant little tree-shaded garden at the rear. I speak with no experience at all of whatever influence it may have on the troops, but must admit that it never occurs to any of us that the institution will acquire the reputation it has since enjoyed, still less become the centre and title of a socio-religious movement.

There are civilian establishments where we feast on egg and chips with coffee and a few other shops. It is refreshing to breathe the air of civilization in between our spells in the not far-distant area of death and desolation.

I have to do another spell of duty in an unfamiliar part of the Ypres Sector when a party of us are sent to relieve some men from another ambulance – not of our division – housed in a dug-out on the banks of the Ypres Canal.

They meet us with a depressing account of the casualties they have suffered. Next morning we learn the nature of the job we have to perform. Our service hitherto has been essentially that of beasts of burden but now, instead of carrying human loads, it appears that we are required to carry what are called "busters", actually cement paving slabs, the purpose of which is to protect personnel from the highly sensitive "whiz-bang" shells commonly used against troops in the area.

They are to be taken to a dressing station in the course of construction and used as reinforcement to be laid on the sandbagged roof. Our route is a communication trench, the name of which sticks in the memory as Threadneedle Street.

On our way to the trench, we pass the dead body of one of our own infantry, left lying apparently where he has fallen. The spectacle is surprising, since this is not no-man's-land nor anywhere near, but no one seems to be doing anything about it. However it is not our business. We shuffle on trying to find the least uncomfortable way of holding the "busters", of which we have one each. The trench is a miserable affair varying in depth from four feet at the most to little more than a few inches where *it has caved in. There are very occasional shelters of a sort covered with corrugated iron, with or without sandbags.*

I mention these details because when we are nearing, as we hope, our destination, we encounter a solitary soldier with news which makes the possibility of cover a matter of no little concern.

His news is that at 11 o'clock, then less than half an hour away, our artillery is due to open up with rapid gunfire in a mock-attack, the object being to induce the opposing artillery to retaliate and so indicate the targets on which our artillery will concentrate their fire.

Apparently all personnel but ourselves in the neighbourhood have been warned to avoid unnecessary exposure in the crucial period. At the dressing station where we dump our "busters", the story is confirmed and as there is no accommodation for us there, we start back without delay. However, undue haste is quite useless. We cannot possibly get back to our own dug-out before the show starts and we know how much cover there is on the way.

In the event, we all get back unscathed. The trench is hit in places as evidenced by fresh damage but nothing but one or two near misses synchronized with our actual passage. A slight hitch in communications has obviously occurred, which could well have resulted in all of us being wiped out while engaged on a less than heroic fatigue, but the incident passes as just one of those things.

9

THE ITALIAN FRONT

Charles Horton was one of many thousands of British servicemen who served on the Italian Front during the First World War, fighting alongside the Italians against the armies of Germany and the Austro-Hungarian Empire. Yet things might have turned out very differently; Italy might well have been expected to fight with the Central Powers, not the Allies.

Italy as such had only existed since 1870, but by no means all Italian states had been included in the new country. Several – including Trentino, the South Tyrol and the Dalmatian Coast – remained under the rule of Austria-Hungary. These detached regions became the source of much resentment and were known as Italia Irredenta, and those campaigning for their incorporation, Irredentists.

Despite this resentment, at the outbreak of war Italy was in formal alliance with the Central Powers of Germany and Austria-Hungary, principally owing to long-term tensions with France. However, when the war broke out, Italy remained neutral since the Central Powers were lined up against Britain, with whom Italy traditionally had good relations.

Once war had begun, both sides openly courted Italian involvement, but after the signing of the Treaty of London on 26 April, 1915, Italy entered the war on the Allied side. Italy had been promised not only Italia Irredenta but also the Ottoman territory of Libya after the war.

The Italian Front ran along Italy's border with Austria-Hungary, for 400 miles from the Swiss Border, over the high Alps, and then down the valley of the Isonzo River towards the Gulf of Trieste. In the Alpine sector, troops fought for high summits and mountain passes from rock-cut trenches often above the snow-line. To the east, on the lower ground, trench warfare of a Western Front character developed. Astonishingly, eleven battles of the Isonzo were fought in order to break the deadlock, but with limited success at most. Almost all of these offensives were launched by the Italians, but in October 1917 the Austrians struck at Caporetto (now Kobarid in Slovenia). The Battle of Caporetto (also known as the Twelfth Battle of the Isonzo) led to a major Italian retreat, most famously described, perhaps, in Ernest Hemingway's novel *A Farewell to Arms*. The city of Udine fell to the Austrians and for a time it seemed that Venice might also be taken.

In the aftermath of the Caporetto defeat, 130,000 French and 110,000 British soldiers were transferred to the Italian Front to help shore it up. Horton's 48th (South Midland) Division was part of this influx. The British mostly took up position behind the River Piave.

Near the end of the war, the Italians, with Allied support, won a major victory at the Battle of Vittorio Veneto and advanced to recapture the ground lost after Caporetto. Austria-Hungary signed an armistice – too late to prevent her empire from crumbling, and Germany was left to fight the Allies alone until it, too, signed an armistice and hostilities ceased on 11 November 1918.

Histories of the First World War often describe the Italian Front as a "sideshow". In fact, it was a major campaign in which the Italians fought with great bravery despite often poor leadership, losing something approaching a million men. Horton and his comrades were not being sent to a relatively safe, quiet sector.

Though we do not know it [yet], our service in France and Belgium is soon to end, and a new chapter in a very different environment and conditions is before us. The Austrians have... launched an attack in Northern Italy and our division is among those to be switched from the Western Front to aid our hard pressed defending Italian allies.

At about the end of September we entrain one morning, this time in a series of wagons each carrying the inscription "Six Chevaux – 24 Hommes" – which are to transport us via Marseilles and the Mediterranean coast to a new battle-front and an unfamiliar country.

The line passes near to Paris, but by that time it is dark and we see nothing. Also, we close the sliding doors of the truck and, having wrapped ourselves in the blankets provided, manage not without difficulty to find just sufficient floor space to lie down for the night.

Conditions are not ideal, but we have known far worse and the noises of the train are much more reassuring than those of the battle areas now well out of hearing. With daylight comes a stop for a sketchy breakfast, equally sketchy ablutions, and attendance to the calls of nature. We roll up our blankets, open the doors, and leave them so during the hours of daylight.

Presently, after by-passing Marseilles, we come in sight of the sea and enter into what is quite our most delightful experience since we have left home. The weather is beautiful, sea and sky intensely blue, the air balmy and scented.

We take turns in sitting in the opening of the truck with legs dangling and thus progress at leisurely speed along that coast which in those days, much more than now, is known to all as the fabulous holiday resort reserved for the titled, the famous and the rich – The Riviera.

Here we are seeing it and smelling it at the government's expense! On our left, rising terraces with villas look like doll's houses, peeping from the trees; on our right, groves of oranges and lemons with sunlit beaches and blue sea beyond. When we pull up for a while, peasant women come up with baskets of eggs, conveniently hard-boiled and sticks of French bread and, if I remember rightly, some English ladies bring gifts of chocolate and cigarettes.

The cities of Cannes, Nice, Monaco, Menton are all on our itinerary, then over the border we stop at San Remo – and we are in Italy. Our train journey ends after dark at a town which turns out to bear the name of Bologna, where we are billeted for the night.

None of us are strong on the geography of Northern Italy or indeed of the precise location of the battle-front and we are not much more knowledgeable after we have spent the remainder of the "duration" there, except for the small area west and north-west of Venice where our marching feet take us.

The pattern of our lives, however, is henceforward to spend our rest times in one or other of the small villages and towns in the extreme northern part of the Venetian Plain, which lies between Vicenza and Padua in the south and the foothills of the Carnic Alps which here form the frontier with Austria.

Going "up the line" means for us climbing the foothills to a height of 1,000 feet to a point known as Tattenham Corner, where the motor road built by the Italians, after many hairpin bends, first flattens out and then slowly descends toward the Asiago Plateau which is no-man's-land.

For a time we remain at Granezza, a location which I have not been able to find in any map and there are no indications that anybody lives here in normal times. It is, however, thought suitable for a sort of advanced Brigade Headquarters and is busy with troops of all branches.

Many huts have been built and others are being constructed. As there is no flat ground, each has to be built on a ramp made of stone, of which there is a plentiful supply. The first "fatigue" I remember being allotted is the gathering of this material, knocking it roughly into the required shape with a sledgehammer, and loading it onto a sledge drawn by a white mule (known as Blanco), operations being held up from time to time by thick fog, in fact cloud, which envelopes everything for a few minutes, before giving way to bright sunshine.

Here too, in the evenings the Divisional Concert Party: "The Curios", play to packed audiences in a large hut. Later some of us are given another stone-cracking job further down the road, where Engineers are blasting an outcrop of rock (while we take cover), following which operation we gather up the fragments and load them on a lorry for removal.

All so far seems very peaceful and congenial, and conditions unbelievably in contrast to those we have left in Flanders. There are constant blue skies, the scent of pines, regular hours of work, and only occasionally the sound of our own artillery or a distant shell-burst to remind us that the war still continues not far away.

When we split up into small groups to man successively the forward posts, it is first at Pria del Aqua, at what we should now call a T-junction in the road at the bottom of a long slope. We hear the old sound of approaching missiles and feel that this is a point well marked on the map for enemy artillery.

After some days and nights of sporadic excitement, we move further forward, turning right into a valley thickly shaded by pine *trees and on to a spot called San Sisto. Here on one side of the road there is a small building which appears to have had a pre-war existence – the first we have seen – but now is so heavily disguised with sandbags around and above that its original function is difficult to discern.*

On the other side a rocky path leads through the trees, following the contour of the rocky ground, wide enough for a man and a mule and leading to our advanced post, a small man-made cave offering shelter to four ambulance men.

I live here for a week or so, but later on have the good fortune to be one of a party of four with the most agreeable assignment that ever falls to my lot. This is to traverse and plot on a map the whole system of paths in this area for the evacuation of "walking wounded".

The path from San Sisto is one of these but continuing the "high road" beyond this point one starts to descend towards the plateau, which could be glimpsed at times through the pines and the strips of camouflage netting now in evidence, threaded through the trees as concealment from enemy observation.

In various spells of duty we see other approaches to the Front. One leads down another valley past "Swiss Cottage", aptly named from its appearance and faced on the opposite side of the road by an encampment of huts, similar to that at Pria del Aqua, where a section of us are housed. Another leads to a village, now in ruins, with odd detached houses sufficiently intact to provide billets and, where the road starts to descend, a large notice announcing "This road to be used in darkness only. Cemetery provided for Daylight Users".

It does not appear that this terrain, then entirely in military occupation, makes any appeal 50 years later to tourists of Italy, who by-pass it on their trips to nearby Venice and northwards to Austria. Yet to us, with recent memories of the devastated plains of

Flanders, it all seems altogether too attractive a part of the world to be experienced under wartime conditions only, in fact ideal for a walking holiday.

As for our long "rest" periods on the plain below, we move around on foot from one village to another as we have done in France and our billets are usually barns. In the hottest part of summer, I remember especially that we live in the upper part of a two-storey barn, the front of which is left completely open so that anyone addicted to sleep-walking is in danger of a drop of ten feet if he walks out in the wrong direction.

As in France we soon discover which cottages are prepared to serve coffee – now café latte instead of café au lait – and something to eat at supper time. Eggs are plentiful and cheap but chips rarer. Instead, we encounter what appears to be almost the staple diet "polenta". This begins as maize-flour boiled to a thick porridge, which having been poured out to cool on a large board, sets sufficiently firmly to be cut into slices with wire, as our grocers used to cut cheese.

The common flavouring is tomato puree – to us as much a novelty as the polenta – accompanied by olive oil or butter and perhaps a morsel of chicken, if available. Not many cattle appear to be grown for meat. The oxen are the principal beasts of burden and we notice a rather charming custom for the families to resort to a space at one end of the cow-byre in the cooler weather and use it as a sitting-room.

Half a dozen oxen provide ample central heating, together of course with a perfume to which only the very fastidious can take exception. Many of the flat fields have long rows of pollarded mulberry trees which serve as supports for wires or ropes to which are strung vines, bearing in summer a harvest of white grapes. The mulberry leaves are plucked to feed silkworms and we are able to see the whole process of silk production in cottage hatcheries.

The wood of the trees is sawn into planks for building and for fuel. We too will use it when, in very cold weather, we sleep in a barn with three walls and our only comfort is a fire which is a tin hat with holes in it. Even when it is burnt the usefulness of the mulberry wood is not finished, for the ashes are used in lieu of soap to make a soaking solution for the washing.

From this, it can be gathered that life for the Northern Italian peasantry is primitive and frugal. They are hardy too, as we notice one morning when a glazed frost makes it difficult for us to stand on early morning parade. Before us at the little stream which still flows freely are the matrons with their thumping-boards rinsing their washing quite happily in the water that is close to freezing in its temperature.

However, I jump from summer to winter and must return to the hot days when to our joy we are free after parade and breakfast to spend our time as we wish. Not far away is a stream artificially cut to irrigate the fields – and at a spot where it turns a corner there is sufficient depth and width for bathing. Undeterred by the absence of any sort of swim-wear, we disport ourselves here each morning, drying ourselves in the sun, with our pleasure marred only by voracious horse flies, which land from time to time and bite into tender parts before we can swat them.

In the afternoon we lie or sit in our elevated billet writing letters, playing cards or bingo or more serious gambling games like Brag and Crown-and-Anchor, according to our individual fancies or, for some, the distance in time from the last pay day. Also we have leave, in batches, to visit Padua or Vicenza, a chance to see town life under more or less normal conditions and the world-famous art treasures, which most of us are never likely to see again as tourists.

When the time comes for us to go up again into the forward area, the most arduous part is the climb up the mule-tracks, far more steep, of course, than the much shorter fine Italian-built motor road with its detours and hairpin bends.

When we are finally installed in the various posts allotted to us, life still bears little resemblance to that in Flanders. Enemy activity has quietened down since the abortive attack which brought British troops to the rescue and on our side it is limited to sporadic harassment by our artillery and occasional infantry raids, heralded by more concentrated shell-fire.

Though I can recall very little stretcher-bearing, we are not entirely spared of anxious moments. The swish of descending shells comes literally out of the blue – for that seems to be the perpetual colour of the skies – and come upon us unexpectedly, usually where there is no cover.

Mostly they burst harmlessly among the trees and rocks. We often have the feeling that with the slightest variation of trajectory, there could be disaster. I remember one incident when a party of us are resuming operations with Canadian axes in tree-felling near the encampment at Swiss Cottage, in which we are billeted. By chance, I am 50 yards away on the other side of the road leading down the valley, when a shell bursts within feet of the working party and one poor chap is left lying with a terrible gash in his face, not fatal, but causing permanent disfigurement.

I am [back] inside the little sandbagged house at San Sisto when it receives a direct hit, but fate decrees that the shell is a small and sensitive one, which bursts on impact without penetrating the roof, as anything heavier would have done.

We follow the infantry down on to the plateau which, during and after our assault, is raked with machine-gun fire and anti-personnel shells. One of the latter misses me by little more than a yard but by luck bursts the other way harmlessly.

It is after this escape that the stretcher party, of which I am one, finds itself, as dawn is breaking, detached from any other troops *and uncertain which way to take to get out of no-man's-land. In both directions are rising tree-clad slopes looking much the same – and we have never before seen them in daylight from below – and I cannot recall what decides us in choosing the direction we do take, but it just happens to be the right one.*

I mentioned earlier the job I was given, with the company of three good friends, of plotting the tracks through the woods, named respectively as the Heart, Diamond, Club, and Spade tracks, for the evacuation of walking wounded. This is undoubtedly the most congenial assignment we experience and whoever thought up this chore deserves our lasting gratitude. We do the job conscientiously, though of course not with professional accuracy, which is in any case not called for, as the tracks are already signposted. We hand in a map which I presume finds its way into the orderly room files and remains there. Happily in our time the tracks are never used for their intended purpose.

We take turns to fetch our daily rations and water – and what cooking is necessary, and tea-making, is done over a primus stove. I remember only one untoward incident which I think is on a Sunday afternoon when we are about to have tea, sitting on the ground in front of the small cave which is our home at the time.

One of those casual shells which remind us from time to time that we are not on an ordinary walking holiday, bursts over a gun battery in front and slightly below us and one of the gunners becomes a casualty, with whom we have to deal. I cannot recall whether we have had our tea, but it sticks in my mind that our pile of bread and butter is stained with the blood of the poor fellow whose wound we have to dress.

Another personal memory of this period of desultory sniping is of acting as guide to a party from another ambulance in the same division who are tasked to follow the infantry, as we have done, into no-man's-land for a night attack. I march with them down the valley from Pria del Aqua to San Sisto and then down the hill to the plateau. Then I make my way back alone. By this time it is dark. I know that the prelude to the attack will be concerted artillery fire from our side, to which the enemy will be likely to reply with particular attention to this important approach road. I am the only traveller and I reflect as I stiffen my pace that anyone hit on this road has little hope of prompt assistance or even discovery. However, I am out of the dark valley and in the welcome company of my friends before the show starts.

When hostilities do flare up, it is the Austrians who take the initiative in another attempt to break through from the mountains to the plain below. At the time we are running a sick-hospital in a village in the foothills and there is an epidemic, a type of influenza, known to the troops as "mountain fever". Many infantry battalions are depleted because of it.

There are a number of victims among our own personnel, myself among them. I am discharged with an allowance of a few days "excused duty" which has not expired when we learn that every man who can walk is to parade for the climb up to the line.

The track is rough and steep in places and takes only a single file and the weather is warm. Soon we are all sweating and puffing profusely, not least those feeling the well-known after effects of "flu", and our morale is lowered by the expectation, said to be official, that we are to go straight into action as stretcher bearers upon reaching the top, and carry on through the night, which is near at hand.

As it turns out, we are treated more kindly by having a few hours of rest, and not having to start our duties before daylight. By this time, the Austrian attack is beaten off and only "mopping-up" operations remain. Our own casualties had been very heavy in the initial attack. We are on duty far into the night but there is no new heavy rush of casualties and our labour in handling what there are is minimized by our having at our disposal, wheeled litters on which to load the stretchers, which we propel with little effort as soon as we are out of the woods and on a reasonably smooth road.

It is raining heavily and our clothing is soaked, remaining so when we finally turn in for sleep in a dug-out after tea and food, wrapped each in a blanket over our wet uniforms. As for me, my post-influenza weakness has evidently been sweated out of me in the previous day's climb, followed as it has been, by a short but sound sleep induced partly, maybe, by a small tot of rum, the first and only time that I accept any part of the ration distributed from time to time on specially taxing occasions.

Our 12 months or so spent in Italy up to the time of the Armistice leave me with few other memories of incidents worth recording and even the names of places we visit in the course of our many moves are blurred. This I think reflects our mood of the period.

The end of the war seems no nearer as one week succeeds another, but we concede that life is much more bearable here, both in and out of the line, than it has been in our earlier years of service, and what news filters through from the Western Front only emphasizes our good fortune in being where we are. The weather seems in retrospect to have been nearly always fine.

There are fresh places to go for our evening egg and chips and café latte. Quite often we are entertained either by our own concert party, "The Varlets", or the divisional troupe, "The Curios", and we play a lot of football and some cricket.

We even have the ambulance sports, but this is on a stubble field with a slope to it, and all our athletic efforts are performed as usual in our army boots. We have a variety of "fatigues", apart from stonemasonry and tree-felling in the mountains and I recall, inevitably, forming one of a party set to clean out some pigsties, both before and after breakfast. We keep fit and healthy and take things as they come.

Sometime in October, I am one of a party detached from the main body of the unit on a project which appears to foreshadow a serious offensive. We set up an advanced operating centre in the grounds of what we would call a "chateau" in France, just outside the substantial town of Treviso, not many miles west of Venice.

This is a new conception in the treatment of casualties, designed to deal with desperately serious cases who might not survive the normal journey to the casualty clearing station, much further away from the line. The idea is a good one, but, in this case, put into operation with such haste and under such conditions that any saving of lives it might otherwise achieve is largely nullified, or so it appears to us, who both set up and staff the hospital.

An operating theatre is improvised in the house, but the wards are marquees which are pitched in pouring rain and furnished with beds set upon the wet grass. Casualties – British, Italian, and Austrian – are apparently far heavier than have been expected.

We, who have to turn ourselves into ward orderlies, have mostly no experience whatsoever in surgical nursing and what little we have learnt in our lectures soon after enlistment is followed with no practice over two years. We do our fumbling best with bedpans and bottles and the difficult dressing of wounds in chest and abdomen. We are competent to supply pills, castor oil, and food to sick patients, but have never before assisted in the application of the vacuum bottle to draw blood from punctured lungs or in bandaging damaged intestines and skulls.

Soon, all the beds are filled and though a high proportion are soon vacated for the mortuary, there is a growing queue of poor chaps left on the stretchers on which they have been brought in, some soaked to the skin through immersion in the River Piave, into which they have fallen, and all desperately in need of immediate skilled treatment, which they cannot have.

Presently, some female nurses join us, positively the first we have worked with, and it is with something of disgust that we see that in deciding which patients could next be brought into the wards, one at least openly puts nationality above need. Perhaps it is necessary, but in our experience of stretcher-bearing under fire, such differentiation has somehow never occurred to us, especially those of strong Christian faith.

We also have a squad of Austrian prisoners to help in the more menial jobs about the centre. They first provide themselves with a place to sleep and do this by wheeling many barrow-loads of earth to cover what has been the enclosed midden or repository of human and animal waste in the years when the estate included farming.

Afterwards, their principal task is preparing the remains of the less fortunate patients for burial. The mortuary is a large marquee and nothing I have seen in France is more depressing than the sight of this fully occupied with rows of bodies awaiting burial. As long as the supply of blankets holds out, these are used as shrouds, but afterwards [they] have had to be hessian. I am given night duty in the wards and, as the rate of loss is reported to be about 70 per cent, there are many changes in the occupants of the beds each time one comes on duty – but always they are men who one knows have but the faintest hope of survival.

The news of the general Armistice on 3 November 1918 should, one might think, be the occasion of ceremonial parades, formal announcements to assembled troops, and celebrations. I remember nothing of the sort.

We who are running this hospital have no parades. Those of us who are on night duty hand over to the day staff as usual and go out for our morning stroll around Treviso before going to bed and it is, as I recall, from the civilian population, that we first hear *rumours that the war is over, though there are no flags and little sign of excitement.*

When we return to the hospital we naturally seek confirmation of the Armistice, and we get it from colleagues, afterwards turning in with the knowledge that the night routine will go on as usual – with wards full and casualties still coming in from the battle that has been taking place prior to the disintegration of the Austrian army.

However, it is my lot to be relieved, quite soon and unexpectedly, of my duties in this depressing atmosphere and transferred to fresh and much more congenial adventures.

10

MISSION TO VIENNA

PROLOGUE

Histories of the First World War tend to focus less on prisoners of war and POW camps, than histories of the Second World War. Yet the International Prisoner of War Agency based in Geneva documented around two million prisoners held in POW camps during the First World War. A few British prisoners were repatriated because of serious wounds or ill health while the war was still being fought, but otherwise, the majority had to wait until release at the end of hostilities – if they could survive that long.

In fact, the Geneva Convention was widely observed and in general prisoners were treated well. British and French prisoners held in Germany suffered along with the rest of the population during the food shortages towards the end of the war, but German and Austrian treatment of Serbian prisoners of war was less humane. British and Empire troops captured after the fall of Kut during the campaign in Mesopotamia (modern Iraq) in 1916 received treatment from their Turkish captors that was perhaps an aberration; forced to march to Baghdad and incarceration, many died of starvation and dysentery on the way.

In general, officers could be assured of better treatment than other ranks, and British soldiers benefitted from Red Cross parcels containing extra rations and other comforts, just as their comrades would in the Second World War. However, Allied prisoners held in Austria and Germany at the end of the war found themselves in a difficult position, released in countries whose regimes were disintegrating and where food was scarce. Many of those held in Germany opted to make their own way to France, often on foot, and there are records of released British POWs meeting bands of German soldiers returning from the former front line and the two groups fraternizing on good terms.

Those held in Austria were much further from Allied territory and unable easily to make their own way home. Missions such as the one Horton accompanied to Vienna were hugely valuable in bringing relief and support to Allied prisoners. It is perhaps unfortunate that Horton did not actually keep a diary of the work in Vienna itself, but his record of the journey through the shattered former front lines and into the heart of a former enemy territory in turmoil is in itself a valuable and fascinating document.

We are running what is known as a corps operating centre and emergency hospital put up in a hurry not far behind the front line to receive the more serious casualties of the great final attack by the Allies entrenched along the Piave River. There have been many casualties on both sides. I have been on night duty in the hospital and afterwards crawl exhausted at dawn onto my bed where I soon fall deeply asleep. It seems like only a few moments later when I feel my body being shaken firmly in the dark room, where daylight is concealed by drawn curtains.

My first reaction is extreme irritation at being woken up after what seems to be just a few minutes of sleep, but this soon changes to astonishment when I realize that my slumber is not being disturbed by a colleague in the billet, or a junior non-commissioned officer, but by an officer.

"Sorry to awaken you, Horton, but the CO needs to talk to you right away and I've been ordered to find you. Get dressed and report to his office immediately. I will accompany you."

As we walk to the colonel's office, the officer explains that the CO needs someone from the unit who can speak German fluently and that he has mentioned my name to the commanding officer as being the only soldier he knows in the field ambulance who is reasonably fluent.

"What's it all about, Sir?" I ask, now fully awake, but still astonished that a mere private soldier is being summoned in person to talk to the colonel in his office.

"I'll let him give you a full briefing, but I can tell you that the CO is to command a small mission to proceed to Vienna and beyond to ensure the welfare and repatriation of Allied prisoners of war. I understand there is already an officer from another unit acting as senior official interpreter, but the colonel thinks it would be a good idea for there to be someone else in the party to help in smoothing out language difficulties among the 'other ranks'."

My selection no doubt arises from the fact that I have been observed frequently talking in a friendly manner in German to a section of Austrian prisoners who are working at the hospital doing the more menial jobs. I have learnt where they come from, the latest news they have about their family, and their hopes for an early release to return home after the Armistice.

The interview with the commanding officer is quite brief – I am offered the job as junior interpreter and told we are to be away across the line in a matter of hours, so I should pack my belongings for a mission that could take months. Our job will be to locate British prisoners of war, nurse them as required, and send back as many as we can find.

Including myself, there are only five RAMC men, the other personnel being motor drivers with a sergeant in charge, all from the Army Service Corps and strangers. No one seems to know for sure, but we are likely to be the first Allied soldiers the civilian population in the conquered territory will see. We are not sure what risk this entails, but none of us worry too much.

Needless to say, I want to get out of the depressing routine of working in a hospital that is being overwhelmed with seriously wounded men. It is exhausting work and I have been doing it for several weeks. I reckon I have done my bit there. Before we leave I write and post a quick letter home to my family in Birmingham explaining in the vaguest terms what I have been selected to do and promising to write regularly.

I reckon this adventure into the unknown will be a welcome challenge and I am flattered to have been selected to take part in this remarkable expedition. In fact I feel almost heroic, as one who has had greatness suddenly thrust upon him. It is the first time my university education has had any bearing on the tasks allotted to me since I have joined the army in 1915. Although, to be fair, I have not chosen at any time to elevate myself from the ranks. I have been content to do my duty without having responsibility thrust upon me.

This mission is especially good for me because it involves saving, not taking life, and so I am not compromised in any way. My Austrian friends, anxious to get news of their predicament to family at home quickly, thrust postcards and letters upon me and I promise to dispatch them if I can find a way to do so.

We leave late at night, unexpectedly, after receiving misleading orders. We have earlier taken to our billets and the comfort of our bed, having been told in true military confusion that our departure would be in the morning at dawn. We are suddenly woken shortly before midnight and told to make our way immediately to the three Fiat trucks loaded with provisions, including of course, medical supplies, tobacco, cigarettes, and matches. Three Talbot ambulances are also in the convoy; all to follow closely on the heels of the retreating and disorganized Austrian army.

I remember feeling it is much the same clear and mild night that I had experienced in early 1916 when our unit crossed the Channel to France from Southampton. We knew then about as much of what awaited us as we do now on this night in Italy. In fact, it is clear within hours of our departure that, as we suspected, we will be the first British troops to be seen in the territory we are crossing.

The roads northwards, towards what has been the front line, are very quiet and we make good progress towards the river. Imagine, if you can, our sensations as we pass through the belt of destruction which up to a few days before has been the combat zone. Roads are still camouflaged, houses empty and more and more of them in a state of ruin as we drive further on, almost expecting to hear the fearful whine of shells overhead, which bring death or mutilation to the unfortunate. It is easy here to forget the war is over. Now we come to trenches, dug-outs, shell-holes, barbed wire entanglements, and finally the river.

At the water's edge we find the first signs of life since leaving civilization. Efforts are being made to repair at last the old permanent bridge which had been blown up by the retreating Italian Army two years before – when its rearguard finally crossed the river and prepared defences on the other side of the Piave.

Meanwhile, all traffic is crossing via a pontoon bridge which, after terrible sacrifice of life, our troops have succeeded the previous week in throwing across the rapid flow of the river in the face of intense Austrian artillery barrage and small arms fire. All is now illuminated by the brilliant rays of searchlights, without which the crossing would be hazardous for large vehicles like ours.

By this time we are on enemy ground and the process by which we have come out of civilization into devastation is reversed. We look expectantly for signs of life on the enemy side of the line where people have been engaged in the ordinary pursuits, as in another world to ours, but cut off for years by a barrier through which no man might pass.

That night, however, the villages we pass through are deserted, though the buildings are undamaged. It is still a long way off daylight when we halt to resume our night's rest in what had been a large Austrian military hospital that is now evacuated, presumably in the chaotic enemy retreat. We are still in Italy and it is not until the following day that we will cross the new frontier.

We depart early the next morning along the dusty road, leaving before dawn, and we soon fall asleep in the vehicles, finding upon waking that we are getting nearer the Carnic Alps. These are a range of the Southern Limestone Alps in East Tyrol, Carinthia, and Friuli (Province of Udine) and are of a blue grey hue on the landscape. They extend from east to west for about 62 miles between the Gail River, a tributary of the Drava and the Tagliamento, forming the border between Austria and Italy.

For most of the day we remain on a course parallel with the mountains and forest slopes, spending the night in the famous provincial city of Udine. The landscape below the foothills is a mix of flat plains and ronchi – the gentle slopes covered with stepped, terraced vineyards where some of the best red and white grape in Italy is cultivated and has been since Roman times.

There is much to enjoy and see here, but I know that with the Armistice just signed there will be no time to do so. I yearn for at least a glimpse of the magnificent Venetian gothic style building of Loggia Del Lionello. There is also the Cathedral or Duomo of Udine, whose interior is completely baroque and containing several important art works from popular artists. The sixteenth-century Venetian castle is located in the centre of the town and Via Mercatovicchio is the cobblestoned main street of Udine, lined with beautiful buildings, villas and shops.

There are crowds of civilians in the city and after wasting most of the day waiting outside Udine, where our officers interview the Italian authorities, we are put up for a second night in a vacant suite of commercial offices. The next day is crammed with interest for we cross a second war zone. It is the area where the Italian advance ran out of steam two years earlier, after their first victorious thrust into the forward columns of the Austro-Hungarian Army. They had taken heavy casualties and then fallen back in retreat to the Piave River where trench warfare took over.

It is a mountainous district where the ravages of shell-fire are nothing compared to those on the Piave. Before we reach there, we pass through villages decorated profusely with flags, streamers, and banners of welcome to the anticipated arrival of the troops of the entente cordiale – they are still behind us apparently. So, to these Italian people our convoy is one of liberation. We do not halt in these villages but drive straight through and are more fascinated by getting our first taste of picturesque scenery.

Just over the Austrian frontier is a wonderful, deep winding valley, where the road is never visible for more than a few hundred yards but seems to get hopelessly lost in the confusion of the mountains, through which there appears to be no passage whatsoever. At the bottom of the valley is a stony river which the road crosses once or twice on high bridges. The roads are strewn with debris of all kinds left behind by the Austrians in their retreat.

At the places where the troops have stopped in their flight to bivouac, there are steel helmets, arms and ammunition, artillery pieces and limbers, clothing and gas helmets lying in heaps. The fleeing troops have sustained severe casualties from strafing air attacks by the Italian Air Force supported by the RAF. We find a use for the gas helmets, ripping out the eye pieces and using them like motor goggles to prevent the dust, which lies inches deep on the road, clogging up our vision. The dust covers us from head to foot by the close of each day.

We also frequently encounter the gruesome sight of the decomposing carcases of dead horses at the side of the road – their flesh has been cut up by hungry and desperate Austrian and Hungarian soldiers craving for meat.

We arrive in our first Austrian city, Villach, at dusk on the day when the Republic of German Austria is proclaimed (indicating the final banishment of the Hapsburgs after 700 years). The new Republic of Austria maintains control over most of the German-dominated areas, but loses various other German majority lands in what was the Austrian Empire. It is clear that food is scarce here.

Villach, inhabited since Roman times near the confluence of the Gail and Drau rivers, is the second largest city in southern Austria, surrounded by various lakes and skirted by the mountains of the Alps. It looks to me more like an English provincial city than anything which I have seen since my leave in the United Kingdom.

We stop in the picturesque main square and are surrounded by a huge crowd of inquisitive onlookers which collect in the course of a few minutes. This is our first experience of being gazed upon curiously, like animals in a zoo – an experience which we get used to afterwards and we hear the following questions again and again in German.

"What nationality are you?"

"Where are you travelling to?"

"What are you doing here?"

"Have you brought foodstuff with you?"

These questions I translate into English for the benefit of the other members in the party, but by the end of the journey, because of the repetition, they are able to recognize them and give the appropriate answers.

The civilians, as well as the city, are remarkably English-looking and in fact most of the Austrians are friendly and in no way hostile towards us. I should mention that except for a .303 rifle and limited supply of ammunition stowed away by each driver, somewhere among the provisions and medical equipment, we are entirely unarmed and in the most ridiculous state of dependence upon the good faith of our late enemies.

Indeed, on the journey itself, our reception at each halt is much kinder than we have expected. We are always being told that Vienna is the place where trouble might be expected and where there has already been bloodshed on the streets following the declaration of the Republic and its separation from Hungary. [However] we are warned there is a risk to our well-being – which adds to the spice of the adventure as far as we are concerned.

We know we are on a mission of peace not war and this can be explained to reasonable people.

In fact, at every place we stop, we find Austrian people who know a certain amount of English as a language and who want to practise it on us – which sometimes amuses us.

"I much English-speaking here," a waiter explains proudly.

At Villach we post the prisoners' letters and change what Italian money we have brought with us, with the kind assistance of a schoolmaster. He guides us to several banks until we find one that will accept Italian paper money and English banknotes. We are by now frequently in contact with Austrian and Hungarian soldiers and at one bank there is a long queue of uniformed men waiting to be served. Some look less than pleased when the foreign soldiers, their enemies, are waved to the front of the queue for service, before them in their own country.

Rubbing shoulders with and chatting to friendly, intelligent human beings, who less than a week before were our enemies and the targets of all the machinery of modern war, is a curious experience. In fact, we take to the Austrians better than we ever have to the Italians. The former seem more self-respecting, as a race more masculine, cleaner and more sincere than we find our southern allies to be.

Yet, owing to treaties between governments, and circumstances which individually we cannot control, we have for a number of years been trying to subjugate one another, using all violent means possible. How senseless and utterly futile warfare is to Christians like myself. I remind myself it was their government that started it. At the same time, we in this expedition do give way to self-satisfied feelings of being members of a victorious army and in fact we take more pride in wearing our khaki uniforms than we have in many months past.

We set out the following day from Villach, late in the morning, and follow the main road eastwards. We are extraordinarily favoured by the weather, which is continually dry during our journey, except for some snow towards the end. We see, in beautiful autumn conditions, one of the most breath-taking features of Carinthia, the southern section of Austria, in the shape of Lake Wortesee [now Lake Wörthersee].

We learn afterwards that during the peacetime years before the war, this is where hundreds of thousands of Austrians would spend their summer holidays. The entire unfolding scene causes me to ask myself how many years it would take me to save up enough money to come here again as a holidaymaker.

The winding road follows the lake for a considerable distance with wooded slopes reaching almost down to the water's edge – and across the lake we can see the outline of small islands. The convoy passes through dozens of picturesque villages. We have dinner at Klagenfurt, our second fair-sized town, and I may say that although we stop at a hotel we provide our own grub. Here, we get news of our first stray English prisoner of war, but we do not find him and he is the only one we hear about until we reach Vienna.

By this time we are well in advance of any Allied troops, which is disconcerting to say the least. While we are still making our way eastwards, we come across a dusty convoy of Hungarian military transport vehicles making its way home to its new Republic. The mile-long column of horse-drawn and motor vehicles in headlong retreat from the combat zone constitutes a strange and pitiful military spectacle, carrying dirty and sullen-looking uniformed men who look exhausted and hungry.

They offer us no threat when they see our British uniforms – indeed they display only a degree of apathy – as we overtake them. The soldiers, some looking like old men, are war weary and have thrown away their rifles and ammunition. We begin to exchange greetings as we pass, a wave here and there, once we are sure there is to be no conflict. They look like what we would expect men to look who are starving, defeated, and making their way through a lean country with a few hundred miles to cover before they reach their Motherland.

We have seen some curious forms of transport in the French and Italian armies but nothing quite like what the Hungarians have left at their disposal. The horses, except for the officers' mounts, are mostly tiny ponies, terribly thin and in a state close to total exhaustion, like the men. Some of the beasts look like they might drop dead at any moment. Most of the carts they pull are about heavy as governor's carts but at least these are pretty uniform – which is more than we can say for their Italian equivalents.

We see a lot of broken-down motor transport on the side of the road and the significant thing we notice is their iron tyres, not a scrap of rubber to be seen on any of the vehicles – our own cars are perhaps a source of wonder to the crowds that inspect us in each town.

The people do not realize how thoroughly they have been beaten until they see our rubber tyres, our cheese, tinned meat, tea and sugar, and other supplementary rations which ensure we are not going to be hungry. We usually have two warm meals, breakfast and supper, and at midday army biscuits and cheese or bully-beef. Whenever we cook our meals the astonishment of the local people at our tea and sugar and full cream tinned milk is unbounded. Our supply of bread only lasts a couple of days, but to those Austrians who have the pleasure of watching us eating it, I think its whiteness is the crowning proof of our victory.

The only fresh meat which we get our hands on during the journey is venison killed by the senior interpreter on the mission in a lovely part of the country where we stay two nights. We are put up at an inn adjoining an imposing country mansion, perched high in the forest and owned, before the war, by an Englishman who had entertained the officer as a house guest in the summer of 1914, before hostilities broke out. The mansion itself is adorned with trophies of stags sporting huge antlers and shot, I suppose, during the last 50 years.

The weather now becomes colder and travelling exposed on the back of the trucks is not the comfortable passage it had been, despite the thick clothing we have piled on. We reach the end of the long ride to the mansion, almost frozen stiff, certainly chilled through and through until we restore the circulation by getting something warm inside us.

In fact, by this time there is snow on the ground. Some of us take turns with a group of Austrian children using their toboggans, but this is not altogether a success as we cannot find sufficiently steep slopes to get decent rides. We end up towing them around the forest paths on foot, which I think they appreciate.

The convoy drives through a town the next day and we stumble across, somewhat to our trepidation, a roadblock manned by a platoon of heavily armed Austrian infantry who halt us with angry gestures and point their guns at us. We are, after all, in what to them are enemy uniforms. There is tension in the air now.

"Halt. Show your Identification Papers!" The suspicious officer shouts at us in German and upon his examination of our papers a barrage of questions follow, demanding to know what we are doing in his country and the nature of our intentions. They seem puzzled we are not Italians. He assumes at first we are the advance formation of an occupying Allied column – if so we are the first entente cordiale forces they have seen. Once we explain we are unarmed and the exact the nature of our business, the atmosphere becomes less tense.

As we get closer to Vienna it is clear the soldiers at the first roadblock have telegraphed our presence to others further along the route. We are stopped frequently by the Republican soldiers, but we encounter no trouble from them. In fact, the best hospitality we receive on our journey comes from some of these officers who have now been informed officially by the military authorities that we are engaged upon a humanitarian mission.

At one place, Graz, near Styria, we are entertained to a slap-up meal and they take us to their heart. We are escorted to a barracks where we are greeted by the officers, those of us who drink alcohol are provided with such, and then we are given a rousing feed of stewed steak, potatoes, and dumplings at the inn next door to the barracks.

They take us to comfortable sleeping billets later that night in a part of the barracks set apart for their volunteer cadets, young men of the educated class who are allowed apparently to serve on special voluntary terms. Here I have an edifying experience, finding myself sleeping in the next bed to a young Austrian who like me is a Christian with strong beliefs. I chat to him about the state of the world for quite a while until I fall asleep.

Among many adventures which happen to us over those few days before we reach the capital city is an opportunity to climb the famous Semmering Pass, within easy reach of Vienna, and a sort of imitation Switzerland, where wealthy people go each year for winter sports. We are late enough in the year to find the pass covered with snow which, though it adds greatly to the beauty of the scenery, makes matters rather hard for our cars, and one breaks down and has to be towed.

We get it repaired at a place called Wiener Neustadt, a munitions' centre and barrack town where the officers consider it unwise to allow us out. We are not to be literally confined to barracks. *After all, are we not the victors? After the Austrians themselves go for a stroll one or two of us decide to follow. The only exciting thing that happens is that we meet the officers coming back.*

We arrive in Vienna after dark one evening, eight days after we started from Italy and we are slightly nervous as to the reception we will receive. Our six cars keep pushing on through the suburbs, however, till at last we come to the city proper and find ourselves in a city which is more like the cities we have left in England than any town I, at any rate, have seen since I was on leave.

Tramcars pass us filled with business people leaving their offices in town, pedestrians, in most English-looking dresses and suits, stop and stare as we drive past them. Taxis and cabs appear, and buildings seem so high – after being long accustomed to tiny village architecture – that their rooftops are almost out of sight.

We finally stop in front of a hotel which is marked in gold letters The Hotel Bristol, where the officers are admitted through folding doors by a footman in uniform.

This may be all commonplace to people who haven't spent a year or two out of civilization but it is a fairyland to us ordinary men. As soon as we stop a crowd gathers as usual around us but, wonderful to relate they are English, voices that greet us, making sure that we are English too. These fellow citizens shake hands with us and hail us as the first English in khaki they have seen since the war started.

Union Jacks come out and all sorts of sentimental things are shouted to us by people who for years have had to smother their patriotism and wait for victory. We never know until this unforgettable moment what it is to have greatness thrust upon us. Now we learn that we are the first British troops to enter Vienna since the signing of the Armistice.

One solitary press correspondent we find has beaten us, but we are the conquering heroes bringing succour and relief to our long-suffering countrymen who over four long years have watched and waited for us in an enemy city. That is how we are received.

In the weeks that follow we learn to know these British people better and find that in their affectionate welcome the fact of bringing foodstuffs plays, perhaps, a larger part than one might have wished. There is in fact a good deal that is cupboard love about it. However, in that first ten minutes we are perhaps happier than at any other time in the war.

It is the exhilarating climax of a wonderful journey and I think we feel in those first handshakes that we are receiving on behalf of the whole British army the gratitude of her exiled sons and daughters. They can hold up their heads again at last and laugh at the enemy who has oppressed them. For us the task now lies ahead of finding, nursing, and repatriating the many British prisoners of war dispersed in various camps.

II

DEMOBILIZATION

We are in Italy for three months working among the prisoners of war, but the job is finally done and we rejoin our unit and endure several weeks in the company of those who are not able to establish urgent claims for release and have to remain as the "cadre" of the field ambulance until the day comes to start the journey to England and demobilization. The process is not hurried.

From Dover we entrain for Blackpool. For the majority of us whose homes are in Birmingham, it is a considerable frustration to halt a few minutes in New Street Station, but to be carried northward without seeing a soul we know.

At Preston we have a two-hour wait on the platform for our connection. It has already been a long day and with nothing better to do, most of us find a seat and doze. A companion and I think the table in the waiting room offers more complete relaxation and we lay ourselves thereon and sleep very soundly. When we awaken, it is to find ourselves alone. The Blackpool train has come in and gone out half an hour ago and we two are the only ones to miss it.

We follow on considerably later and obtain directions to our allotted billet, which turns out to be a tiny house in one of the meaner streets of the health resort. Though we have a bed to sleep in, for the first time in three years – not counting leave now 18 months gone – we fail to register any great thrill at the experience.

There follows ten days of frustration, parading each morning, queuing for uninteresting meals at a one-time skating rink and in between hanging about to have any kit deficiencies made good, and afterwards handing the lot in, and finding what compensatory enjoyment we can on the promenade in the evenings. Then we entrain again, but still not for home.

For our demobilization papers, we have to go to Chiseldon on Salisbury Plain, passing once more through the Midland capital and retracing much of the ground we have already traversed from Dover.

Eventually we are through the last formalities and are civilians again to find our train for the last journey home. On the station platform we say farewell to those of our number who hail from Bristol or Gloucester and thus informally sever connections which in some cases had been very close – and are never to be renewed.

The Birmingham party splits up again at New Street with a few more handshakes before we trail off singly to our various buses and trams, each to make his solitary entrance via the familiar roads to the familiar home.

A few months earlier I have seen in Germany large streamers across the street proclaiming "Welcome Home to our Returning Warriors". The British way is different. We just drift back, change into our civilian clothes, and begin the task of taking up normal life again where we have left off.

LATTER DAY REFLECTIONS...

Those of us who survived service in the First World War... are able to compare – albeit as civilians – the second conflict a generation later. While much more terrible in its devastation of life and property in the home lands of the warring countries, the war of 1939–45 differed perhaps above all in being a war of movement instead of attrition. In the Second World War the fighting soldier was spared the unimaginable horrors of months and years of trench warfare which their fathers endured between 1914 and 1918.

That broad fact is, one supposes, understood even by the new generation of schoolchildren, but with all the records now available from both sides of the strategy of both wars, and the casualties, there appear to be surprisingly few first-hand accounts of life as it really was for the common serviceman in France and Belgium in the "Kaiser's War".

Whether in prose or poetry, most first-hand records of experiences and emotions on infantry service are the work of officers. As to the fighting, no one can question their right to speak; the mortality figures and the Rolls of Honour of schools and universities pay their said tribute to the young men who went from OTCs to take commissioned rank and lived but a few months.

However, the common soldier who shared the risks of his superiors without their responsibilities, suffered living conditions which for most of the time were distinctly inferior to commissioned men, but which have seldom been described in print and hardly ever in book form. Yet the roughness of sleeping quarters and food, the discipline and physical labour, including long marches under heavy loads, the lice which infested his dirty clothes, were all part of the cross the private soldier had to bear and which should be taken into account as part of his war service and sacrifices.

In these respects, the field-serving rankers in my own branch of the army, the RAMC were little better off than their fighting brothers. Our food was the same, usually adequate, but mostly from tins and never interesting, always cooked in field kitchens, which meant a smoky trench fire, water tasting of chloride, of lime or petrol, or both – it came either from the water-cart direct or via petrol cans – and consumed without benefit of tables or chairs.

Butter came out of tins and was often rancid and whilst I have mentioned "Maconachies" and bully-beef among the staple canned diets, I should not omit to refer to the even more ubiquitous pork and beans. These were the precursors of the new popular baked beans, from which they differ mainly in their lighter colour and less marked flavour. In the top of the tin there was to be found, on careful examination, a piece of fat pork, the size of which was so nominal that half-way through the war, the story went round that Simcoes, the American makers, had killed another pig! Apart from flatulent attributes, which they shared with all other beans, I have nothing against them and recall many occasions when they made an acceptable supper – an unofficial meal at which we ate whatever we could scrounge.

Normally the ground covered was the same for all of us; when the brigade or the division moved from one area to another, we moved with them, though our spacing before we started and when we reached our separate destinations, might account for a couple of miles more or less.

On our longest marches we would start after an early breakfast at around 8 a.m. and finish in time for a late tea, having had ten minutes rest in each hour and one longer half-way.

Most long treks as I recall were in fine, warm weather, causing such copious perspiration amongst some individuals that the upper part of their tunics turned from khaki to black. The singing with which we enlivened the first few miles died away well before the end and our march became little more than a shuffle in which we let one leg move after the other in time with the pair of feet in front of us.

However, having reached our new billet, cast off our packs and harness, lined up for our mugs of tea and whatever food the cooks had to offer, our exhaustion passed away with remarkable speed. Nothing like a shower or other means of a complete wash down was, of course, ever available, but we performed what ablutions we could and spruced ourselves up. Some had to attend to blistered feet, but few found it necessary to take any prolonged rest. For further proof of the resilience we were able to command, it was no uncommon sight to see a football brought out within half an hour of our arrival and being kicked about on whatever bit of flat ground happened to present itself.

Whatever our tough life did for us, it certainly made us fit. When one has humped around 40 or 50 lb all day, it is astonishing how light the feet feel when the load is discarded. In the evening there was of course some exploring to be done. We seldom landed in a town of any size but we had to find the location of the estaminet or trattoria or a house where it was possible to get coffee and egg and chips, as individual fancy dictated. Settling down in our new beds was noisy but cheerful and insomnia was not one of our afflictions.

I suppose it could be said that we had developed a sort of philosophy or code to cope with our way of life, though no doubt this varied according to the widely different temperaments to be found amongst us. Some degree of fatalism was common to all, as more relevant than mere optimism or pessimism, and this largely ruled out introspection, the attempt to analyse our own feelings. I imagined each man's unconscious desire was to prove that whatever came our way he could "take it" as well as the rest. This could account for the absence of any great amount of grousing or moaning.

Besides which "belly-aching" was in any case a useless waste of those precious periods of safety. However we did not scruple to give vent to our real feelings in a whole series of songs on the march and in our billets.

A number of our songs came undoubtedly from the music halls of the day. The marching we did in England before going abroad was enlivened with some of these, such as "Hallo! Hallo – Who's

Your Lady Friend?", "Keep the Home Fires Burning", "Hold Your Hand Out You Naughty Boy!" and similar jingles and, of course, "Tipperary".

The last named seemed to have passed the peak of its popularity when we reached France, maybe because we unconsciously felt it belonged to the original Expeditionary Force, maybe that constant repetition had worn it threadbare.

Current hits with a mournful note in them, like "All Dressed Up and Nowhere to Go" and "When I Leave the World Behind" sung andante, seemed to strike a sympathetic chord towards bedtime and from time to time we learnt that some new attractive jingles from current London musicals through the Army Concert parties.

The mood of men separated from their sweethearts and wives, and indeed from feminine associations of any sort (except one) naturally favoured the heavily sentimental love-songs, like "Give Me Your Smile", "When Irish Eyes are Smiling", and "You Made Me Love You", which appeared to differ from the pop songs of today in having memorable tunes and therefore still find considerable favour today in the programmes of the (formerly Black & White) Mitchell Minstrels and Olde Time Music Hall.

I could mention a few other tunes of that time, in the same genre, which equally appealed to us but have unaccountably been missed in the revivals. It was the whole string of songs of completely anonymous origin, which remain most strongly in the memory.

Most of these can only be recorded here in heavily bowdlerized version. Indeed the more squeamish amongst us did our own bowdlerizing in joining in the singing on marches, rather than hold entirely aloof from these sometimes very catchy tunes. Here again a few have been given a airing in the recent film, Oh! What a Lovely War, *the title of which came from the song which began as follows:*

> *Oh, oh, Oh it's a lovely war.*
> *Who wouldn't be a soldier, eh? Oh it's a shame to*
>   *take the pay.*
> *As soon as reveille has gone we feel just as heavy*
>   *as lead,*
> *But we never get up till the sergeant brings our*
>   *breakfast up to bed!*

This had a good marching tune, but whatever the metre, we could render any part of our repertoire and still keep in step.

> *I want to go home, I want to go home.*
> *I don't want to go to the trenches no more.*
> *I don't want to hear the artillery roar.*
> *Take me over the sea, where the Allemandes can't*
>   *get at me.*
> *Oh my, I don't want to die, I want to go home.*

"You'd be far better off in a home!" went to a regimental march-tune, but our version of the words can hardly have been the original. Having repeated the first line, it continued:

> *For your King and Country need you,*
> *But the blighters they won't feed you.*
> *You'd be far better off in a home.*

The many parodies of popular hymns were mostly in the same vein of anti-patriotism. For instance, we sang to the tune of the Sunday School hymn, "We are but little children weak":

> *We are but little soldiers weak*
> *We only earn five bob a week.*

The more we work the more we may;
It makes no difference to our pay.

And to the tune of "The Church's One Foundation":

We are Fred Karno's Army,
The R A M C (T).
We cannot fight, we cannot shoot,
What ruddy good are we?
But when we get to Ber-lin
The Kaiser, he will say,
"Ach! Ach! Mein Gott,
What a ruddy fine lot
Are the R A M C (T)."

While a well-known revivalist chorus became:

Whiter than the whitewash on the wall!
Whiter than the whitewash on the wall!
Oh wash me in the water that you wash your
* dirty daughter in,*
So that I can be whiter than the whitewash on
* the wall.*

A surprising feature of the purely nostalgic ballads that we fancied was that they were nearly all about somebody else's homeland (e.g. Ireland in the case of "Tipperary") but one exception was, of course,

Take me back to dear old Blighty!
Put me on the train for London town!

Take me over there,
Drop me anywhere,
Birmingham, Leeds or Manchester, well,
I don't care!

I should like to see my best girl,
Cuddling up again we soon shall be,
Hi-te-iddley I-tee,
Carry me home to Blighty,
Blighty is the place for me!

However, in the next breath it was not "Blighty" we wanted to get back to but Arizona, Tennessee, or Michigan. Otherwise we were goin' to "My Home in Dixieland". These, of course, were the days of ragtime, an importation from America which swept England and which we gladly took with us to France. The syncopated rhythm appealed to us and the sentiments expressed in the words by Negro cotton pickers, cowboys, or settlers usually, like us, far from home, definitely struck a chord. Here are a few samples of the lyrics from memory:

In Arizona, there's a ranch in Arizona
That is the place where I long to be.
Someone dear waits for me,
In Arizona, there's a girl in Arizona
Who loves me – very tenderly – very patiently,
I wish I could go – back again you know,
Back to Arizona – where the girl waits for me.

I want to go back, I want to go back,
I want to go back to the farm.

Far away from home, with a milk-pail on my arm.
I want to be there, I want to see there
A certain someone full of charm.
That's why I wish again
That I was in Michigan,
Down on the farm.

Back home in Tennessee
That's where I want to be,
Right by my mother's knee,
She thinks the world of me,
They'll be dreaming to-night
Of the fields of snowy white,
Darkies singing, banjos ringing,
All the world seems bright.
The roses round the door make me love Mother more,
I'll see my sweetheart Flo
And friends I used to know.
They'll be right there to meet me.
Just imagine how they'll greet me
When I get back, when I get back,
To my home in Tennessee.

Way down on the levee in Old Alabamee
There's Daddy and Mammy, there's Ephraim and Sammy
On a moonlight night you can find them all.
While they are waiting, the banjos are syncopating,
What's that they're saying, what's that they're saying
While they keep playing a humming and swaying?
It's the good ship Robert E. Lee,
That's come to carry the cotton away!
Hear them shuffling along, Hear their music and song

Demobilization

Go take your best gal, real pal,
And go to the levee, I said to the levee,
And join that shuffling throng, hear their music and song.
It's simply great mate, waiting on the levee
Waiting for the Robert E. Lee!

Marriage of Bert to Lilian Florence Hooper,
Handsworth, Birmingham, 1922

12

BERT IN CIVILIAN LIFE

The present-day Horton family is not sure what Bert decided to do after the war, when he came back to Handsworth, but we can assume he wanted to put his degree in commerce to good use and may have opted in the early years to manage the administration of father Joseph's freelance news agency in New Street, Birmingham, specializing in business and industrial journalism in Britain's second city.

Bert's older sister Nellie and his younger brother Arthur had both been working in Birmingham with Joseph for some years while he was away serving with the RAMC. Arthur, an expert transcript shorthand writer who worked in the courts, was later awarded with MBE for his services. Birmingham in the 1920s was certainly an exciting city in which to be a journalist and a well run agency could expect to make good profits – such was the appetite for news round the clock.

The regional papers like the *Birmingham Post* and the Wolverhampton *Express and Star* – which also covered the Black Country – had several editions coming out through the day and it was the same for the evening papers like the Birmingham *Evening Mail*. Competition among the Birmingham daily newspapers was intense, and competent freelances knew that less than 120 miles away Fleet Street was also hungry for good editorial material every day. It was a golden age for freelance journalism.

No audited documents remain to tell us how successful the agency was, but Joseph died at the age of 68 in 1928 after a career in journalism spanning over 40 years. At one time he had edited *The Labour Tribune* and was later chief reporter of *The Birmingham Argus* before going freelance. He was a prominent member of the Institute of Journalists and is likely to have passed on to Bert his knowledge of the iron, steel, and non-ferrous metal markets. Joseph had been the British Correspondent of *The Iron Trade Review* published in Cleveland, Ohio.

Music played an important part of the life of the Hortons – Nellie and Arthur learnt piano. Nellie was a particularly competent pianist and in modern times could possibly have made a professional career of being a musician, but she lived at home by the late 1920s, looking after her mother, who was by now a widow. Nellie continued to work in the family business office but she did not venture very far. None of the present-day Hortons know at what point the agency was either sold or ceased to operate.

They all attended the Francis Asbury Methodist Church in Handsworth on Sundays and their faith was very important to them. Later they also attended the City Road Methodist Church in Edgbaston, where Bert was a circuit steward and sidesman.[6] Bert was an active member of the tennis club at the church and also its drama group. He enjoyed playing leading roles in its productions. Years later in the 1950s his grand-daughter Angela can remember attending productions when she was a child, seated on the front bench in the church hall and feeling very proud of her grandpa disguised as various characters.

In 1922 Bert married Lilian Florence Hooper, whose parents owned a hairdressing business. Bert's brother Arthur, who was a pianist and a very able organist, played at their wedding. In March 1925, Lily and Bert had a daughter, Eileen Mary. Mary remembers a happy childhood, despite becoming an only child; when Mary was five years old, another daughter was born but she unfortunately died of meningitis after four months.

Sometime during the 1920s Bert became a senior member of the support staff at the Birmingham Chamber of Commerce. This would most probably have brought him into contact with the city's leading business and political figures of the day. Birmingham was no longer the powerhouse of the Industrial Revolution as it had been in the nineteenth century, or "the workshop of the world" but it was still the "city of a thousand trades" and as the "second city" was hugely important as a centre of British industry and commerce. Every sector was strongly represented. There were thousands of large factories sprawled across the West Midlands' conurbation and even more light engineering workshops employing a handful of men.

Birmingham was the home of many well-known national figures who were prominent in business circles. These included men such as Neville and Austin Chamberlain, Leo Amery, Herbert Austin, Egbert Cadbury, Oliver Lucas, Sir Alfred Owen, Joseph Sankey, James Norton, Colonel Edward Ansell, and George Lanchester. We will never know how well Bert knew them but they were all involved with the Chamber.

As a former freelance journalist, Bert would also have known the City Council's leading socialist councillors and aldermen and a succession of Lord Mayors from 1930. Birmingham and the Black Country was a hotbed of militant trade union activity by the early 1930s and the growing influence of the Communist Party meant its hand could be detected behind many of the strikes by aggrieved working people, especially as the Great Depression deepened and poverty manifested itself.

As a Nonconformist Christian, Bert was a believer in social justice for the working man, but his descendants can only speculate where his real sympathies lay politically in a time of ongoing industrial unrest.

They stress that he was a private man not given to airing his political views, but as an avid reader of the John Gordon column in the Tory *Sunday Express* it is unlikely that he was a socialist. There are certainly hints, however, in his war memoirs that he had scant respect for the ruling classes whom he held largely responsible for the pursuit and then conduct of the catastrophic war. Perhaps he played his cards close to his chest when dealing with the industrialists of Birmingham. It would have been in character if he did. On leaving the Chamber in 1935, he was presented with a glass cabinet – which his daughter still has – which suggests fellow members of staff at the Chamber held him in high regard.

In the mid-1930s Bert worked for the National Union of Mineral Water Manufacturers based in Birmingham and edited its journal. An important post came his way in 1943 when he was asked to set up the Union's London office and he and the family moved to London. His daughter Mary worked for him as his secretary and she remembers the office was on the corner of Oxford Street and Duke Street and faced the threat of the V1 flying bombers during 1944.

The family cannot recall how Bert came to be linked with the Union but his religious beliefs could provide us with a clue. The British government believed the uninterrupted supply and consumption of non-alcoholic beverages were vital for both morale and the war effort. There was even a Parliamentary Committee set up to supervise the running of the industry, which lost tens of thousands of men during the war when they left their jobs to join the armed forces.

There were thousands of small companies manufacturing soft drinks like lemonade and ginger beer up to the time of the Second World War. Many of these family-based companies had been in business since the mid-Victorian era and had thrived because of the poor quality of tap water. Bert never drank alcohol apart from perhaps a glass of sherry at Christmas or a tot of rum if he had a cold, and his strong religious views meant he was well aware of the evils of excessive alcoholic consumption – so working for the soft drinks industry would have been in harmony with his beliefs.

The multinational brands like Schweppes, Coca Cola, Corona, and Britvic were already around but the manufacturers of still mineral water in plastic bottles were still years away in the future. The American brands had become even more prominent with the arrival of US forces in Britain in 1942.

Most small towns had at least one soft drinks company and the provincial cities would have had several firms competing with one another selling lemonade, ginger beer, and orangeade. For the most part these small companies operated on a local or district level and few had the capacity or vision to develop into national brands.

Many companies closed down for the duration of the Second World War, due to a shortage of labour and their delivery vehicles being commandeered by the military. The trade was now controlled by the SDI (Soft Drinks Industry). The business of the closed firms was taken over by the few larger companies left operating. Those had to pay money to the SDI and this was divided amongst all companies that had closed down. It must have been a challenging time for Bert, presiding over the interests of a widely dispersed industry, but one that needed to be kept going to underpin public morale and provide an alternative to alcoholic refreshment.

London was not an easily accomplished move for the Horton family during the war, even though they chose to live in the suburbs in Orpington, Kent. Mary remembers the family became part of the congregation at the Methodist Church in Sevenoaks Road. She recalls many disturbed nights while bombers overhead dropped bombs on their way home towards the coast. In 1945, Bert developed a skin condition on his hands and his daughter Mary recalls her mother, Lily, bandaging his hands. On the advice of a specialist they returned to Birmingham because London was considered bad for the condition.

When the Horton family moved back to Birmingham they lived in a house in Devonshire Road, Handsworth Wood, and it was from here that Mary was married to Peter Emerson during the month of September 1946, shortly after the war.

By this time Mr Hooper, Lily's father, had died and left her a hairdressing business and shop in the centre of Birmingham. Bert decided to take over the management of the Hoopers Bros business in West Bromwich. This involved importing hair from Italy for the wig-making department together with handbags and glassware which were sold in the shop. He also tried his hand at making hair treatments and ran the businesses until the lease ran out.

Bert and Lily moved to Sutton Coldfield to live just in time for the birth of their first grandchild, Elizabeth Anne, who was born in July 1949. Mary and Peter had bought their first home in Sutton Coldfield, too, so Bert and Lily played a big part in the lives of their grandchildren. Bert's interests by then included gardening and he built a pool in their garden.

He still enjoyed amateur dramatics at Asbury Church, in Handsworth, became secretary of the Metallic Bedsteads Association (for hospital beds), and later worked part time for the Prisoners Aid Society. Bert was very capable domestically, could cook well and nothing was too much trouble around the house, helping to care for Lily who had heart trouble and did not enjoy good health.

Angela and David, two more grandchildren, were born in 1952 and 1956 respectively. Bert and Lily were very much part of the family life – joining in with birthday parties, holidays in Wales, Sunday lunches, and services at the local Baptist church where Mary and Peter were members. Angela said: "There are many photos to remind us of happy occasions in our childhood with our grandparents whom we called Nanny and Bampa."

Elizabeth remembers Bert teaching her to swim in a freezing sea at Towyn and taking them out in a pedal boat at Blackroot Pool, Sutton Park. She recalls:

> *He was very good at mending things, like soldering saucepan handles on to very old saucepans – the make do and mend of the war years I think. He loved his food and I can see him after a good Sunday lunch sitting back and lighting his pipe. He always seemed to have a twinkle in his eye.*
>
> *I remember him being very proud holding Andrew, his first great grandchild. Also, he gave us a lot of advice about our first garden and lots of cuttings from his garden. I used to enjoy going to his home and playing the piano while he was on the violin. He would get his old favourite pieces of music out and I would have to sight read. Sometimes I can remember thinking the violin sounded a bit squeaky but in fact Bert was an accomplished musician and played in the Sutton Coldfield Light Orchestra in the late*

60s and early 70s. I think the music gene has
been passed down through him to us all.

Lily died in 1959 at the age of sixty-two, and Bert, although very lonely to start with, made a life on his own and looked after himself very well. By now he was retired, still actively involved with the drama group, however, making props for them out of plaster of Paris – things like pork pies and fish. He was very clever with his hands despite the skin problem. He continued to enjoy painting watercolours.

Grand-daughter Angela:

> *He had a challenging mind and always did the*
> *"skeleton crossword" in the* Sunday Express
> *and loved reciting monologues to us like "Albert*
> *the Lion". He kept budgerigars and had a go*
> *at breeding them. We grandchildren would be*
> *quite amazed when we went up to Grandpa's*
> *house to tea and the budgies would be let out of*
> *their cage allowed to fly around the lounge!*

He enjoyed holidays on his own or with friends, mainly in Britain, but he did fly to Ireland. He loved Llandudno in North Wales, particularly, where he had spent time as a young man with his parents.

Bert kept in touch with a few army friends. One was George Allen and they played chess together and shared a pub lunch occasionally. He was famous for reminiscing about the army in the First World War after church on Sunday with his family around him.

Angela recalls:

*I can remember after lunch he would sit down
with his pipe and tobacco, and tell tales of his
youth. We were probably not very good listeners
and I wish we had paid more attention.*

*Later, we all enjoyed watching comedy on
TV and two of his favourites were Arthur Askey
and the inimitable Tommy Cooper. We would
listen to* Round the Horn *on the radio after
lunch on a Sunday and in the evening watch the*
London Palladium Show.

He enjoyed playing a big role at the weddings of both Elizabeth
and Angela and, in particular, presenting grand-daughter Angela
with "the key of the door" and a speech, as her wedding day was
also her twenty-first birthday in August 1973. She says:

*In 1975 Mary and Peter moved to Exeter in
Devon, and Bert had the opportunity to go
with them – however he decided not to uproot
himself at this stage of his life, but to visit as
much as he could.*

*He was still able to see his grand daughters
who lived not far away in the Midlands, and
also David, who went to live with him for
a brief period while he was completing an
apprenticeship in Birmingham, before joining
his parents in Devon.*

*In 1976 after spending three happy weeks
in Devon with my mother, Mary, and father,
Peter, he returned home to Sutton Coldfield and
developed a chest infection. On 19th October,
just two days before his 81st birthday, he*

collapsed and died on his own upstairs, just before going to bed. Bert was found the next day by Arthur, his younger brother, who lived nearby.

APPENDICES

This section of the book does not deal with the non-combatant career of Bert Horton but is intended as an educational guide explaining the military structure in which he served as a member of an RAMC field ambulance unit. It includes a description of conditions endured by men living in the trenches.

Appendix 1

STRETCHER BEARER'S WORLD

Enduring images of the Western Front during the First World War include lines of opposing trenches, massive artillery bombardments, and armies advancing across a shell-scarred no-man's-land under heavy fire. During offensives, shell-bursts, shrapnel, machine-guns, and rifle fire resulted in a considerable number of casualties, but British soldiers were ordered not to intervene to help any comrade who was wounded. This, of course, went against the deepest instincts of those involved, both as soldiers and as human beings; many published memoirs of the First World War describe harrowing incidents where veterans recall their anguish at having to leave a fallen friend behind.

It was the job of the regimental stretcher bearers to bring casualties back to the British lines. These men were drawn from within their battalions and at fraught periods would be augmented by further volunteers. It was a dangerous role, carried out right in the battle zone, and stretcher bearers did not carry arms. This aspect of the role appealed to those who, owing to their convictions – often Christian or socialist – did not want to take life but who wished to serve in the line. One such soldier was Lance Corporal Bill Coltman from Burton-on-Trent, a member of a Brethren church, who became the most decorated British non-officer of the war. He served as a stretcher bearer in the North Staffordshire Regiment and among his medals was the Victoria Cross.

Regimental stretcher bearers were the front line link in a lengthy chain down which the wounded were evacuated. Soldiers who were hit took whatever cover was possible, treated their wounds as best they could (every soldier carried a standard field dressing) and waited for rescue by the stretcher bearers. When wounds were sustained during a quiet phase of trench warfare – a soldier being shot during a trench raid on the German lines, perhaps, or being hit by a sniper – there would usually be little delay before the casualty was collected by regimental stretcher bearers. However, during a major offensive such as the Battle of the Somme, casualties were often so numerous that stretcher bearers would be overwhelmed and the chain of evacuation became congested and overloaded. In these circumstances, the wounded might have to wait for long periods, often in considerable pain, before they were attended to. Many who lay wounded in no-man's-land died before help came. Those who were able might try to crawl back to the British lines, or at least to a shell-hole or other place that offered protection; shell-holes, of course, could be treacherous during wet weather, and particularly during the Passchendaele campaign, many men slipped into deep shell-holes and drowned.

Regimental stretcher bearers served in no-man's-land behind the advancing troops and their immediate task was to return wounded men to the regimental aid post (RAP) commanded by the regimental medical officer (RMO); who was usually an RAMC Lieutenant or Captain. RAPs were close to the front line in a sheltered location such as a dug-out, communication trench, building, or even a deep shell-hole.

The theory behind medical treatment of the wounded was that it should start as soon, and as near to the front line, as possible. However, front-line units could only ever provide basic medical treatment. As their name suggests, RAPs specialized in first aid at a level that was designed to return lightly wounded men to the fighting as rapidly as possible. If the injuries were more serious, the casualties were passed to an Advanced Dressing Station or ADS, the next link in the chain.

When casualty levels were exceptional, further staff could be attached to the RAP. In addition, the RMO could sometimes call on RAMC stretcher bearer teams from a field ambulance unit (like the one to which Horton was attached) for front-line duty. On the other hand, if the pressure on the RAP was light, the RMO might himself move into the battle zone to tend to the wounded on the spot.

An effective, well-run RAP was essential to the handling of casualties during an offensive, and to the morale of the soldiers who received treatment there. The RAP could draw on a wide range of equipment, drugs, ointments and dressings, which were supplied by nearby ADSs, but it had little space and no capacity to hold any number of wounded men. Casualties who required further treatment were moved on to an ADS by the RAMC stretcher bearers. Inevitably, during an assault, many of the wounded would have to wait, perhaps lying untended on stretchers, before they received further treatment.

The ADS might be housed under canvas or in a substantial local building if one was available, and would usually be located near the reserve trenches. Ideally it would be about 400 yards behind the RAPs so that it was within reach of the walking wounded and stretcher bearers loaded with a casualty. In ideal conditions, two RAMC men could easily carry a casualty on a stretcher, but in wet weather the weight of the burden could double; four men might be needed to carry a wounded man across saturated ground. Stretcher bearers like Charles Horton needed strength as well as courage. Crossing broken, muddy ground can require considerable effort for anyone, but the bearers had in addition to try to avoid rocking or abruptly moving the stretcher and so increasing the pain and discomfort of the wounded soldier. In extreme cases, the jolting of a man in great pain could bring about death from shock. Stretcher bearers often underwent such harrowing experiences and it was not a job for the squeamish.

Both RAMC and regimental stretcher bearers had one of the most onerous tasks facing anyone on the Western Front. The rest of the army had great admiration for them because, since their work required them to attend to casualties on the battlefield, they were always called to the most hazardous locations. The RAMC men acquired a heroic reputation for their willingness to volunteer for any job, however dangerous or unpleasant. John S.G. Blair, a historian of the RAMC, described stretcher bearers as "the most important men in the whole Medical Services of this Great War".

During an offensive, teams of RAMC stretcher bearers would be dispersed across miles of ground that was impassable for motor or horse-drawn transport, delivering the wounded to the next link in the chain. In some cases they might end up carrying a casualty as far as four miles, much of it across difficult, shell-torn ground. Stretcher bearer relay posts were established to try to avoid long carries.

A field ambulance of the kind in which Charles Horton served was a mobile front line medical unit that organized several links in the chain of evacuation, including the relay posts, walking wounded collecting stations, dressing stations, and rest stations. When Charles Horton was in the front line in July 1916, relay posts for stretcher bearers were established roughly every

1,000 yards. Some communication trenches were designated specifically for removing casualties to avoid congestion during the heat of battle. During these times of heavy fighting, such as the early stages of the Battle of the Somme, the various posts could be overwhelmed by the numbers of incoming casualties.

The main dressing station (MDS) would generally be a mile or so further from the front than the ADS. Here, wounds could be dressed and some urgent operations undertaken. The journey to the next link in the chain, the casualty clearing station (CCS), was generally made by motor ambulance, especially later in the war.

RAMC Captain Noel Chavasse VC was an RMO in the First World War who became one of the most decorated members of the army's medical staff. He corresponded regularly with his family back in England and the following letter describes an attack in April 1915 during the early days of trench warfare, before Bert Horton arrived in France.

> *We went up to the trenches from which we were to jump up on the night of the 14th. It was an eight-mile walk, and the pipers played us for four miles. There was a tremendous stream of men along the road, as a whole brigade was to attack. The men were in the best of spirits, and sang all the way. My stretcher-bearers who had had their number increased to 24 [were] making as usual a joyful noise, and had finally to be silenced by the Adjutant. We halted at last, for we had to go up to the trenches by a by-path, and I said Goodbye to as many Officers as I could. I had been ordered to stay back on a main road half a mile behind the trenches, and felt very sore about it, but I went up to see what the ground was like.*

*At 2 a.m. a terrific bombardment began,
and went on till 4 a.m., but I was so tired that I
dozed through it. But at 5 a.m. I was woken up
by the first batch of wounded coming down. They
came along a long communication trench in a
steady stream. Meanwhile the Huns began to put
crumps and shrapnel down the road. Our C.O.
arrived with an artery bleeding in his head,
which was troublesome to stop, and we had to
lie him down at the back, as a crump landed too
near the dressing station for safety. Then news
came that a Captain Cunningham was lying
exhausted at the top end of the communication
trench. So he had to be fetched down. I then
found the trench blocked with men who had
dropped exhausted trying to drag themselves
along. The Huns were putting big shells into
the trench, and making direct hits, so that in
places the trench was blown in, yet not a single
wounded man was hit all day. It was a weary
job helping poor Cunningham down the trench.
He was hit in the leg and arm, and was very
brave. We got some more men back at the same
time, but when we arrived at our place we found
that another crump had burst just outside our
dressing station, and wrecked it, and had killed
four men next door.*

*When I got out of the trench it was getting
dusk, so I went off with a trusty man, and
searched for the wounded. I knew where the
charge had taken place. We found most of them
in a little coppice. They lay behind trees, in "dug-*

*outs", and in the bottom of trenches. They were
so weak that they could not call out. Their joy
and relief on being found was pitiful, and fairly
spurred me on to look for more. It was awful work
getting some of them out of their trenches and
"dug-outs". It was hard to find men enough to
carry them away. I had to appeal for volunteers
for the men were dead beat. Finally, at dawn, we
got our last wounded away from a very advanced
point, at 4 in the morning. Altogether, we had
collected 18 men behind the trenches, and were
pretty well certain that none were left.*

A readable account of the dangerous job carried out by stretcher
bearers during the First World War was published by Little,
Brown and Co. of Boston in 1921. *Letters of a Canadian Stretcher
Bearer* takes the form of a series of letters written by R.A. Ray,
a Canadian soldier, to his wife, Lallie, back in Canada. It was
originally published anonymously in 1918. Ray wrote as follows
to Lal, as he called her, on 9 May 1917.

*Dear Lal,
I don't know how much you know over there
about the recent fighting. I mean of this past
week. I have a hunch, too, that letters from
here are going to be pretty closely censored for
a week or two, so I'll be careful, as I want you
to get this.*

*We arrived yesterday [out of the line] at
daybreak. This morning I had my first wash and
shave, and though feeling horribly "dopey" I'm
much better than I was. We've had a "strenuous"*

trip, very strenuous. Some of the old-timers say it has had the worst of the Somme beat. All admit it was as bad. Some one is looking after me alright. Never a scratch. I cannot believe it, and there is no doubt whatever that at least on one occasion I was in the very hottest corner of all...
Our bunch were to go up on a party to dig a new front-line trench – our two sergeants were getting the turn together – when a big one fell almost on top of them. I think I've mentioned Mike to you. I doubt if we could have had a better sergeant. He was a real friend to me, a stranger in the Company; helped me in every way. Every one liked Mike. It happened about twelve feet from me. He was walking along the trench, had just passed my funk hole with the other sergeant, when the shell came. I felt it must have got them. I went out. Only S. was alive; he was terribly hit. Another stretcher bearer and I did what we could. I didn't see anything of Mike. There wasn't enough of him, I heard afterwards, to see. We got S. on a stretcher, and I helped get him out; but he died before we got anywhere.
All the time we kept hearing we were to be relieved, but always they told us "tomorrow". One night, I was in the front line to continue it another hundred yards; that was a cinch. All we had to contend with were snipers. We didn't have a casualty. Next day, Fritz slowly moved up and down over it in a plane. Whenever there was a bunch of men hunched rather close together, he dropped a flare. The same second over came

a shell, and – no trench – no men. I was in the trench the next night, beyond it to our other Company to get out the wounded. All the way, we climbed over dead bodies.

The salient is like a horseshoe. The heavies come in from in front, the light from near-by behind. The trenches are not trenches, only two feet or so wide and about four feet deep. Fritz has every inch marked. These poor men – Why should it be them *that line the trenches? I leave you to imagine what it's like, getting a wounded man out. The stretcher is wider than the trench. One night, we got on top to carry; we stayed about a minute. The first flare to come over, and he got after us with both whizz bangs and heavies. Right there is where a miracle occurred. A shell dropped amongst us and – even now I don't understand it – it never went off. Not one shell in a thousand does that now. Well, we got out. Our stretcher cases were alive, and our "walkers" too. Going down the main trench, he shelled us all the way. It was the night of the relief, and we passed them coming up. Imagine that, too, if you can. The men hurrying, cursing, with sobbing breath, coming up; and we were trying to get down with our stretchers. Telephone wires across the trench everywhere. I dunno' how it's done; but it is. When we got to our own part of the trench, another party took the cases and went on out. Our relief came about the same time. Our troubles weren't over yet, though. Fritz, of course, was wise to the relief, and, going*

*out, in addition to ordinary shelling, put up
a gas barrage (shells) away back. This we had
to pass through. He threw a fearful lot, and it
was pretty bad. However, we got through that,
too. And, like a lot of drunken men, arrived at
the point – some miles away – where our cook
wagons were. I forgot to say that it rained. Here
we flopped in the road, and ate steaks and drank
tea – then slept. Then, came the really interesting
part of the night. We'd been asleep awhile, when
were waked up to "stand to". Fritz had come
over on those trenches and taken 'em. Now can
you beat that? Personally, I couldn't either think
or move, I was so "all in"…*

*One thing you said in your letter – that you
supposed I would get hard and all that, through
this thing. Well, the exact opposite is the case. The
sight of this continual killing and wounding is
making me madder and madder at such waste. I
have even got where I wouldn't kill a mouse or a
bird, if you paid me. It seems ridiculous maybe,
but that's how it is with me at present…*

*We are the goats. The fellows who really want
the thing are miles and miles away from the shells
and the hardships. They know they will live,
whereas I don't know I'll even live to finish this
letter. After it's over, they win anyway – because
we have lost years or months of happiness, and
our health in any case impaired for good. The
old times had it all on us. Their kings led 'em
into battle, and took a chance, too. Yet if I hadn't
come, I'd have despised myself forever!*

CASUALTY CLEARING STATIONS

The casualty clearing station or CCS was the first link in the chain of evacuation that resembled a large, well-equipped medical facility. They were usually located at least twelve miles behind the front line, roughly midway between the trenches and the rear or base area. A main railway line for the evacuation of casualties was usually nearby and there would be good connections by road to the front line area as well as an abundant water supply. The CCS was the furthest forward unit that was equipped and prepared for surgery and was also usually the most advanced location where nursing staff were stationed. Even so, the treatment they could provide was still limited.

Only serious casualties, those who could not be safely moved, remained for any length of time at the CCS; soldiers with minor wounds would be treated and returned to their units, while the majority were transported by rail to base hospitals or to the coast for evacuation to hospitals in the UK. On some occasions, such as during the Battle of the Somme in 1916, CCSs struggled to cope with the unexpectedly large numbers of casualties.

CCSs were necessarily large operations and occupied up to half a square mile of ground. They usually took the form of tented camps, although there might also be semi-permanent huts. Usually there were about six medical staff and perhaps the same number of nursing sisters. Sometimes CCSs would be situated so that two or three were grouped fairly closely together near a convenient railhead. A CCS could generally care for around 1,000 patients, but during major offensives they were often overwhelmed. Major emergency operations such as limb amputations would be carried out by RAMC surgeons in CCSs.

There were attempts to co-ordinate the work of CCSs. One might be operating as normal, treating casualties for evacuation to base hospitals, while another nearby would be free of patients and being prepared to receive new casualties. A third might only be involved in dealing with illnesses, but would be able to evacuate these to make room for battle casualties in an emergency.

If there was a particularly lengthy journey between the front line and the CCS, additional field ambulances were stationed en route so that the casualties' wound dressings could be checked, though they would only remove the wounded from the motor ambulance for immediate treatment if it was absolutely necessary.

By September 1917 there were fifty-nine CCSs on the British sector of the Western Front; at the height of the Passchendaele battles in late 1917 there were twenty-three serving the Ypres Salient alone. During every year of the war, hundreds of thousands of men on the Western Front were treated at CCSs and evacuated from them. Many could not be saved. Larger Commonwealth War Cemeteries in France and Flanders today often mark the sites of former CCSs.

THE WIDER ROLE OF FIELD AMBULANCES

Field ambulances were RAMC units but most of them operated under the command of an army division, with each division usually having three field ambulances. In such a setting, each field ambulance had a special responsibility for looking after the casualties of one of the division's brigades. When the division was seeing action, two of the field ambulances would be in forward positions while the third was held in the rear.

A typical field ambulance would be staffed by ten officers and 224 other ranks. In theory, each field ambulance had the resources to cope with 150 casualties, but during major offensives they would be swamped by the volume of incoming wounded.

Even right at the end of the war, the army relied to a large extent on horse transport and the field ambulances were no exception. At the start of the war, a field ambulance would have ten horse-drawn ambulance wagons but by the end of 1914 each was also supplied with seven motor ambulances. The use of motor ambulances increased throughout the war, though they never entirely replaced horse transport.

The field ambulance was the RAMC unit that operated closest to the front line. It was also the first link in the chain of evacuation where the casualty's name would be recorded and details of his injuries and treatment documented. A field ambulance consisted of a headquarters section, which formed an MDS, and two more sections which deployed forward to form two ADSs. These sections were further divided into; the "tent division", which included the medical staff and incorporated the area where casualties were treated, and the "bearer" division, including stretcher bearers.

Horton was usually in one of the subdivisions involving stretcher bearers responsible either for collecting casualties from the RAPs, and carrying them back to the "tent division" at the ADS, or manning the relay posts. Later in the war, fully-equipped surgical teams served in ADSs so that urgent operations could be carried out closer to the front line.

The Hospitals

From the CCS, casualties who required further treatment were evacuated, usually by train, to a base hospital far from the front line. Captured German wounded also often made the same journey by rail. There were two "stationary" hospitals for each division within the army. The chances of a British or, indeed, German soldier surviving their wounds were generally good if they got as far as a hospital. Stationary hospitals could hold up to 400 casualties while the general hospitals could take over a thousand.

The term "stationary" hospital is misleading as these facilities could be moved to a new location more easily perhaps than, say, a CCS could. Sometimes they were used as specialist hospitals, focusing on, for example, victims of poison gas or venereal diseases. They often occupied the premises of a civilian hospital in a large city or town.

General hospitals were usually located near railway lines to ensure the speedy transfer of casualties from the CCSs, or forward to the Channel ports for returning casualties to the UK. Hotels and other large buildings were often requisitioned for general hospitals, though some occupied hutted camps. In their functioning they resembled civilian hospitals, with the same departmental organization, administrative systems and resources. Bacteriology and X-ray units were also attached to the general hospitals.

Well over half of the men admitted to hospitals were subsequently transported back to England for further treatment or convalescence in any of hundreds of hospitals and nursing homes located throughout the UK. There were also some convalescence units in France itself for the recovery of the less seriously injured.

Medical care in the army developed significantly during the war. Realizing the quicker the treatment, the more likely it was that the casualty would survive, the system of casualty evacuation described here was established and continued to evolve. As the war went on, it demanded a massive increase in the recruitment, education, and training of doctors and nurses.

Ironically, just as the war encouraged developments in engineering and communications technology, it also promoted advances in medical care. The use of saline drips to prevent shock and the number of blood transfusions both grew during the course of the war, and standards of hygiene were also greatly improved. Perhaps most significantly, there came some recognition of the psychological effects of warfare, as what was originally termed "shell-shock" became identified as a genuine neurosis that required treatment.

Many wounded soldiers longed to be evacuated to the UK, to the extent that they coveted a "Blighty one" – a wound that did not permanently disable but which was serious enough to ensure that the casualty would be returned home and discharged from service. Men who were returned to the UK for treatment, especially if they were able to visit their families, naturally hoped to be released back into civilian life. However, most patients received their treatment and then were eventually cleared for further front-line duty.

Appendix 2

LIFE IN THE TRENCHES

The early clashes on the Western Front took place in the context of a war of movement in which armies marched and advanced and manoeuvred and attempted to outflank each other and met in set-piece battles. However, by Christmas 1914 the front lines had stabilized behind formidable defences and further movement was frustrated. A line of opposing positions, separated by a strip of no-man's-land, ran from the Belgian coast across northern France for 450 miles to the Swiss border.

Trenches were dug to protect troops from machine guns, rifle fire, and shells. However, along some parts of the front, it was not possible to dig. In wet, low-lying parts of the front, such as Flanders, standard trenches would often simply fill with water, so instead defences had to be built up into breastworks using sandbags and other materials. At the other end of the front, in the Vosges Mountains, French and German positions often had to be cut out of the rock.

There were usually at least three lines of trenches, the one nearest to no-man's-land being the main fire trench or MFT. The successive lines of trenches were linked by communications trenches built so that even when proceeding towards or away from the front line, soldiers were under cover. Only when out of firing range could military activity be undertaken in the open.

However, as the war drew on, the range of artillery increased and danger from air raids became more common.

Early trenches had what were called "funk-holes" – narrow openings in the side of the trench perhaps screened by a length of sacking – for soldiers to rest when off-duty, but in time larger "dug-outs" were constructed in both rear and forward trenches. Some of these were large and elaborate, but rarely as comfortable as those the Germans were able to construct. A typical dug-out would be provided with wooden bunks along the walls, one above the other. There were blankets and straw in the bunks, most of which were crawling with lice, one of the unavoidable discomforts of life in the front line. Ideally, each dug-out would have at least two entrances, in case one was blown in by a shell.

The front-line trenches usually had a parapet built of sandbags and wood protecting the edge nearest no-man's-land and the enemy, with a corresponding parados on the rear edge. There would be a firestep at the base of the forward wall so that the soldiers could raise themselves in order to aim their weapons across no-man's-land. There would usually be wooden duckboards on the floor of each trench to prevent the build-up of mud and increasingly elaborate buttressing, revetting, and strengthening of the trench structure to keep it from collapsing.

Soldiers sent into the front line did not spend all of their time fighting in battles. In fact, surprisingly little time in the front line was spent in actual combat except during the major offensives. Instead, the soldiers would be assigned to work such as filling sandbags, repairing or strengthening trenches, and so on. Some areas of the front line had reputations as "quiet sectors" where there was little artillery or sniper activity and the opposing soldiers informally adopted a "live-and-let-live" philosophy. Such an attitude was frowned upon by senior officers in the British army who tried to maintain "the offensive spirit" by encouraging small actions, such as trench raiding parties to capture prisoners or reconnoitre the opposition defences. Sometimes British and German patrols would meet in no-man's-land, and either hurried on their separate ways or engaged in hand-to-hand fighting. The use of handguns on night patrol in no-man's-land was forbidden because it could draw machine-gun fire. So, the hand-to-hand fighting would be basic and brutal, involving spades and clubs.

The line of trenches ran through fields, woods, towns, and villages and each setting presented challenges to those constructing the trench network; trenches on higher ground, looking down at the opposing trenches, conferred an advantage. Large trees or surviving buildings in the trench region might provide places for snipers to threaten opposing front line troops.

Between the lines of trenches, the two sides formed great barricades of barbed or razor wire which made successful assaults even more difficult. Another form of work that troops were often set was laying out new barbed wire entanglements or repairing damaged ones. This work was always carried out at night and it was not unusual for British and German wiring parties to meet unexpectedly in no-man's-land.

Trenches were not dug in straight lines, but rather in zig-zags or toothed patterns so that if the trench was occupied by enemy troops they could not shoot straight along the trench; it also meant that when shells or bombs burst near the trench the blast was partly contained.

Shallow trenches called "saps" were dug at intervals leading beyond the wire into no-man's-land. These might be used as jumping-off points for offensives or as a means of accessing listening posts or machine-gun positions. Both sides employed teams of miners to tunnel beneath no-man's-land so that large amounts of explosives or "mines" could be placed beneath enemy trench systems and detonated in advance of infantry assaults. Several such explosions were, for example, triggered before the Battle of the Somme in 1916 and the Battle of Messines Ridge in 1917. The explosions were often enormous and left vast craters in the landscape, many of which can still be seen today.

The distance between the two opposing front lines varied from as little as thirty to forty yards to a more normal several hundred yards. When an enemy front-line trench was captured, consolidating it involved a lot of physical labour; the parapet and firestep would be facing the wrong way, for example, and would have to be changed. This procedure was known as 'reversing' a trench.

As early as December 1914, when the tough, professional regular soldiers of the British Expeditionary Force were experiencing the extreme pressures of trench warfare after perhaps seventy-two hours in the line, Captain Noel Chavasse VC noticed that, since they were young men, they were able to recover quickly at this early stage of the war.

> *Our men have had a terrible experience of 72 hours in trenches, drenched through and in some places knee-deep in mud and water. To see them come out, and line up and march off is almost terrible. They don't look like strong young men. They are muddied to the eyes. Their coats are plastered with mud and weigh an awful weight with the water which has soaked in. Their backs are bent, and they stagger and totter along with the weight of their packs. Their faces are white and haggard and their eyes glare out from mud. Their short bristly beards give them an*

almost beastlike look. They look like wounded
or sick wild things. I have seen nothing like it.
The collapse after rowing or running is nothing
like it. Many, too many, who are quite beat,
have to be told they must walk it. Then comes
a nightmare of a march for about 2 to 4 miles,
when the men walk in a trance… and in about
3 days, they are as fit as ever again.

Many British soldiers kept a diary of their experiences of life in the trenches although, in fact, they were not supposed to do so. The surviving diaries often paint a vivid picture. Thomas Fred Littler joined the Cheshire Regiment in 1914 shortly after he turned seventeen, and signed for foreign service on his eighteenth birthday. As a private soldier, he left England for Rouen in March 1916 and went over the top with his battalion on 1 July 1916, the first day of the Battle of the Somme. The following extract records his experiences of the day, and of the month leading up to it.

June 6th 1916
We had to pack our kits, and proceed up the
line, we passed through Bayencourt, and then
in artillery formation to Sailly-au-Bois, and
from here we marched in single file along a very
muddy road, where in places men sank knee deep
in mud, at last we reached the ruined town of
Hebuterne, 400 yds from our front line. There
are no civilians here as the place is subject to
heavy fire every day. We were billeted in the
cellars of an old farm house which was minus a
wall and the roof.

I took a stroll round the place after tea and found it absolutely ruined. A church at one end had been badly battered and the walls all smashed and the roof gone, one side of the tower standing only. A noticeable fact was that a crucifix in a most conspicuous place remained untouched.

June 7th 1916
We left our billets and went to the edge of the village, moving under cover of the broken walls. We entered a communication trench called "Yale Street" and moved along this trench in daylight for 300 yds. Now we were only 100 yds from our own front line, and 400 yds from the enemy front line. This "com" [communications] trench was in places only 3 ft deep, and we were exposed to the enemy fire, and our own work was to deepen this trench to 7 ft, also make it wide enough for two men to pass. No earth could be thrown on top, but had to be put in sandbags and passed down the trench.

Everything went well 'till 3 o'clock in the afternoon when "Jerry" started to strafe, and strafed us away from the work, and managed it without any casualties. During the time we were working we had to keep our equipment on, also rifles at hand. Leaving the trench we looked "rum cutters" being covered with mud and clay, all around the place were "gas alarms". This day was the first time I had been close to the enemy lines, and the first time I had got as far as a Support trench.

June 8th 1916
We worked in Yale Street trench again, also in trench 48 which was much deeper. Our artillery opened up at about 10 a.m. There was a heavy strafe on the enemy trenches and in reply the Germans shelled us heavily. There being no dug-outs here we were compelled to stick it, and chance our luck. There were no casualties, but four men got buried and had to be dug out. They were badly shaken. Later a shell dropped on the parapet above four men and one had his leg blown off. The trench was wrecked and we were compelled to move down a little way.

June 9th 1916
We fell in at 8.30 p.m. and entered "Wood Street communication trench" and passed the old fire trench. Then we went up "New Wood Street" which was only about 2 ft deep, then got on the top, passed our front line held by "The Rifle Rangers", through a gap in the barbed wire. We were paced out so many paces per man as a digging task, and told to dig ourselves in as quickly as possible.

We worked hard for about half an hour when the Germans opened heavy machine gun fire on us and swept us like a blanket. Being only 100 yds from the enemy lines it proved very trying. We carried on, off and on, for a quarter of an hour until the enemy got more machine guns sweeping that sector. By this time my part of the trench was about 18" deep so I could lie in it.

The machine guns keep on sweeping and the enemy opened out a "miniweffer" (trench mortar) barrage, four of our rifles were laying on the ground about 4 ft away and these got a direct hit. That was the last I saw of my rifle. This barrage also blew the trench away and left us as if we were on the open ground.

The man in front of me called for help. On going to him I found he had a piece of shrapnel in his left shoulder blade… He was also hit on the lower middle part of the back. Many men at this time were calling for help and out of our platoon we had three casualties. These were L/Cpl Fineflow, who was hit in the back, his lungs pierced with shrapnel. He was vomiting a lot of blood. Pte Edward Coalthorpe of Chester was hit in the ribs and left arm. One man in No. 10 Platoon was also hit, Stretcher Bearer Mostan; he was serious as he was hit in the lower part of the stomach and between the legs. After we had got the wounded away, we returned to billets at 6 a.m.

June 10th 1916
We worked from 11 o'clock in the morning until 2.45 p.m. when we returned to our billets. We fell in again at 8 p.m. and worked

on top in the same place as the previous night and returned at 2 a.m. We had one casualty, this being the Corporal Brooks who was hit in the right wrist, the centre of the wrist being blown clean out.

During the night a shell burst and mud and stones flew all around and I had my knee cut through, being struck with a stone. It was Whit Sunday morning.

June 11th 1916
I had my knee dressed by the Medical Officer, went to work in the Com trench, returned at 2.30 p.m. without a casualty and mounted guard at 4 p.m. We heard of the Russian advance on the Eastern Front.

June 12th 1916
I dismounted guard at 4 p.m. and had to go out with the company same night. We fell in at 8.30 p.m. and returned at 2.30 a.m. wet through to the skin with rain. In places the trenches were knee deep with water.

June 13th 1916
We worked from 10 a.m. to 2.30 p.m. in a CT [communications trench] called Woman's Street which was close up being at the end of Dead Man's Wood St. We carried on again from 9 p.m. to 11.30 p.m., when the enemy gave us a heavy trench mortar strafe.

This gradually got hotter and one mortar dropping on the parapet over us completely buried three of us. We were dug out and taken to the first aid Post and medically examined and found to be suffering from shock. We returned to the company next morning much better but a bit shaky.

June 14th 1916
I returned to the company at 10 a.m. and this afternoon two more men were buried in a dug-out. One was Private George Shaw of Chester who joined the Battalion the same day as me. He was killed, having both legs blown off. The other, Private Lol Beasley of Runcorn, had one leg blown off and was just alive when we got him out. I mounted guard this afternoon until 4 p.m. the following day.

June 15th 1916
We paraded at 7.30 p.m. and dug on the top from the front line support to the fire trench; this new CT was called New Yiddish Street. The night was quiet except for a little machine gun fire, and we returned to billet at 3 a.m.

June 16th 1916
We laid trench boards in "New Yiddish Street" from 10 a.m. till 1 p.m. and at night paraded at 9 p.m. and dug a new ambulance trench from Yale Street to the new fire trench. The moon was full and the night very light and

we were on the end of heavy machine gun fire for 20 minutes. Afterwards the night was very quiet. Second Lieut. Larne of our platoon was wounded in the ribs and legs by the machine gun fire.

June 17th 1916
We turned out at 11 a.m. to work but had to return at 12 noon as Yale St was being heavily shelled. We had a draft from D Company sent to us as our company had got so weak from men going to hospital with wounds and sickness. We paraded at 9 p.m. and passed up Calvary St, but had to wait a while as the Germans were shelling the woods heavily through which the trench passed.

Whilst waiting, a shrapnel shell burst overhead and one man, Private Joe Orme of Runcorn, was hit in the face, the bottom lip being torn off and bottom teeth knocked out. Afterwards, we worked in "Young Street" running off the end of "Calvary Street". The night on the whole was quiet, but one of the reinforcements from D Company was killed being shot through the head with a machine gun bullet.

June 18th 1916
We worked as usual both morning and night, but all was quiet and we had no casualties.

June 19th 1916
This morning each man had two boxes of hand
grenades to carry up to the front line trench and
then we came back to billets. In the afternoon
B Company came up to Hebuterne to relieve us
and we marched back 10 kilometres to Souastre.
When passing through Sailly-au-Bois and
Bayencourt I noticed all the civilians had left
their homes since we went up.

June 20th 1916
We left Souastre and marched through Henu and
Pas to Grenas, a village about 10 kilometres from
Souastre. Here we were still within sound of the
guns and we were out for rest – and training for
an offensive.

June 21st 1916
I did Sanitary Corporal's work for the company,
and did a journey to Pommera, a village midway
between Halloy and Grenas.

June 28th 1916
Stood to until 2 p.m. then marched 10 kilometres
back to Souastre, passing through Pas and Henu;
Souastre had changed a little as most of the
civilians had taken refuge farther away from
the line. We also heard of the death of Corporal
Brooks who I previously stated as having been
wounded; also we had many orders read out to
us as we were to advance at the hour of zero in a
day or so.

June 29th 1916
We stood to all day to move up but did not. The
bombardment in the line was increasing every
day and was now practically continual.

June 30th 1916
EVE OF BATTLE
We stood to till 4 p.m. when we handed in our
packs and all personal effects and started for
the line, going forward in artillery formation.
The Company passed through Bayencourt,
and Sailly-au-Bois up to Hebuterne. The
bombardment on German positions was more
fierce than before and we knew we had to attack
in the morning. The minutes seemed like hours.

July 1st 1916
After having had our rum issue we stood to till
7.25 a.m. when we put up a smoke screen and
went over the top at 7.30 with the London
Scottish and Queen's Westminster Rifles. We
took four lines of trenches from the Germans,
but were driven back by midday to our original
position. Our losses were very heavy although we
took many prisoners.

The casualties from my Battalion were A
Company 112, B Company 62, C Company
91, D Company 25. In my platoon we lost 10
out of 30 men: Lieutenant Leigh, who had
taken over from Lieut. Larne, was wounded
with the left arm blown off; Private Harry

Wakefield, Private Wilfred Carter, killed;
Private Jack White, Private Frank Walker,
missing, and Private Harry Frodsham, Private
Sam Mellor, and Private George Parker
wounded, L-Cpl R Eaton, and L-Cpl Harry
Carveley wounded. The following men died of
wounds during the succeeding week: Sgt Piers,
L-Cpl J Kinsey, and Private Albert Clarke,
Private Jack Perrin, and Private Sidney Jones.
We left the line this night being too weak in
numbers to hold it, and got back to Souastre
about 12.30 pm.

July 2nd 1916
We rested all day, and many of us are still a
little shaky.

When there was no offensive in progress, much of trench life was routine. No soldier could leave his post without the permission of his immediate superior, and an officer had to approve him leaving the trench. One officer from each company was on trench duty at all times, and his sergeants and corporals had to report to him on an hourly basis. He was required to patrol his assigned trenches, checking that the equipment was in good condition, that the sentries were alert and that the men were as comfortable as possible.

The men were woken an hour before dawn with the morning "Stand to" during which a section or platoon would be posted on the firestep with bayonets fixed to repel any dawn raid by the enemy. At dawn, machine guns, shells, and handguns would be fired towards the Germans to make sure they knew that their opposite numbers were on the alert.

After the pre-dawn "Stand to", rum was issued while rifles were cleaned before an inspection by officers. Men could then prepare their breakfast, with fried bacon, bread and tea being the great favourite. Breakfast marked an unofficial truce between the two sides on the live-and-let-live principle but again some senior officers made units open fire on the enemy line to create tension.

After breakfast, the duty commanding officer would begin his inspection, a ritual that was largely a weapons check and an opportunity for ordinary soldiers to speak. Then the daily work tasks were assigned and carried out. Movement was restricted in the trenches for the bulk of the day. Snipers and observation posts from either side constantly scanned the line and shots would be fired when any activity was visible. The rounded steel helmets that are now such an iconic symbol of British and Empire soldiers during both world wars did not come into use until early 1916; before then, soldiers just had their field service caps or, for Scottish regiments, bonnets, and were particularly vulnerable to snipers.

When the opportunity presented itself, many soldiers caught up on sleep, while others wrote letters home; surviving letters, like diaries, have become valuable documents in the history of the war. Some made ornaments or useful items from used shell and bullet casings, items now known as "trench art". Pieces of this kind can often be seen on television antiques programmes and some fetch large sums at auction.

Dusk brought the second "Stand to" of the day. Afterwards, in the dark, the trenches came to life and both sides were acutely aware of each other's activity. Under the cover of darkness, the men fetched food, water, and maintenance supplies, while others were sent to the firestep for sentry duty. Two hours was regarded as the limit before they were replaced, in case they fell asleep. A soldier who fell asleep on duty might be executed by firing squad.

Darkness was also used as cover for changing over front-line troops. Those who had completed their front-line duty were swapped with fresh troops from another unit. A typical trench routine was four days in the front line, followed by four days in close reserve and finally four at rest, but this would vary enormously depending on conditions, the weather and the availability of reserve troops. In close reserve, perhaps based in a trench system just behind the front lines or in a ruined village or wood, men had to be prepared to return to the line at short notice.

The soldiers in the trenches ate reasonably well, and the food was often a good deal better than what they or their families back home were used to. Rations, of bread and jam and biscuits and butter and a variety of tinned foods, were fairly generous, but many memoirs of the war speak of the ever-present bully beef, "Maconochie's" – a brand of tinned stew with vegetables – and plum-and-apple jam. By contrast, Fray Bentos, still familiar today, was a widely-trusted brand of tinned meat dishes.

Hot prepared meals were served in the trenches, but only when there was no ongoing offensive and they could be delivered from the field kitchens. During a battle it would not, of course, be possible to have set meal times.

During the course of the war, the design of trench systems developed so that they became formidable fortresses with extensive barbed wire entanglements, concrete shelters and emplacements, and machine guns permanently trained on gaps deliberately left in the wire. By 1918 some defensive systems, particularly on the German side, extended several miles back from the front line.

Tall men were at a distinct disadvantage in the Allied trenches and had to keep their heads down at all times; trenches were supposed to be six feet deep, but in battlefield conditions they would often be much shallower and vulnerable to sniper fire. In winter, the wooden duckboard flooring was frequently flooded with dirty, evil-smelling muddy water.

One of the characteristic smells of the trench system – one that soldiers never forgot – was the reek of human excrement. Latrines had to be dug close to hand and generally were as a deep a hole in the ground as was possible, over which was mounted a plank to sit on. Sometimes a sap would run backwards from the front-line trench and end in a latrine. Men would, with permission, leave their post to use the latrine and most preferred to do so in the dark. Latrines were often a particularly cruel target for enemy snipers and shell-fire. They were also a considerable health hazard.

Scraps of discarded food, overflow from latrines, empty tins, rotting dead bodies, the engrained dirt of living in the trenches, the inability to wash or change for days or weeks at a time and many other discomforts meant that there were severe health risks completely unrelated to combat. The ubiquitous nuisance of lice has already been mentioned, but disease was spread by rats and by the maggots and flies that thrived on the nearby remains of decomposing human and animal corpses.

The weather was a dangerous and formidable enemy particularly when it caused trenches to flood. Men suffered from exposure, frostbite, and "trench foot", a wasting disease of the flesh caused by wet, cold feet being constrained by boots and puttees, for days on end. Trench foot could cripple a man. The feet would gradually become numb and the skin turn red or blue. If untreated, trench foot could turn gangrenous and lead to amputation.

In winter, soldiers did their best to keep warm, especially at night. Experiments to create heating in the dug-outs were unsuccessful. Braziers that burned smokeless fuel were placed outside in the trenches, and could be used for cooking, but were often difficult to keep alight in bad weather. Standing water in the trench system – annoying in the summer – became life-threatening in the winter.

The noise and bustle of a change of front-line units increased the risk of attracting enemy attention in the form of shelling, machine-gun fire or even a raid at the very time when the unit were changing over. Once the incoming unit was settled, various precautions would be taken. At least one man in four at night, and perhaps one in ten by day, were posted as sentries on look-out duty, perhaps in saps forward from the MFT.

Generally, however, except when a major action was underway, trench life was often very dull and involved hard physical work. Officers had to try to balance the need to contend with the enemy, the need to build and repair defences and the need for rest and sleep. Routines, schedules, and timetables were essential in this. Offensives and counter attacks disrupted the routines, but these formed a surprisingly small proportion of time in the trenches.

Besides those in the opposing trenches, the main enemies of the soldier on the Western Front were the weather and boredom. If boredom led to loss of concentration, so leaving oneself exposed to sniper fire, it could be fatal.

Appendix 3

NON-COMBATANTS CITED FOR BRAVERY

The life of a soldier as described in Appendix 2 developed because, for over three years, the 450-mile line of the Western Front rarely shifted more than a few miles in each direction, and so in each set of trenches a strange, temporary society was created, with its own enormous system of support industries and services spreading back to the rear. At least part of the continuing fascination with the First World War is this curious long-term deadlock which has no parallel in history. Yet the techniques and methods of trench warfare – communication trenches, saps, tunnels, and mines – were nothing new, having been part of siege warfare for centuries. Trench systems were formed by forces laying siege to castles during the Cromwellian era and towns, such as Mafeking, during the Boer War. There were trenches in the Crimean War, the American Civil War and the Russo-Japanese War; digging for cover was something British soldiers were trained to do, and well used to doing, long before 1914. But it is the sheer scale of the Western Front trench systems, and the completeness of the deadlock that continues to puzzle and fascinate. How and why did it happen?

In some senses, the trench stalemate on the Western Front was almost inevitable. In the years leading up to the war, artillery fire had increased greatly in its destructive power and attacking troops also faced additional hazards from the development of machine-guns and high-powered rifles. The only option when faced with such a storm of fire was to dig in and go to ground. Infantry assaults became costly and more difficult to direct successfully. The armies actually worked hard to increase firepower in order to smash through the trench systems, and in response the trenches themselves became deeper, more elaborate, and more difficult to eradicate. Stalemate developed, and not just on the Western Front; for example, it was also a feature at Gallipoli and on the Italian Front.

Before 1914, the military on all sides had prepared for a war of movement. The Germans had planned a swift descent on France through Belgium, resulting in the capture of Paris and French surrender, so that they could turn their attention to the Russian threat on the Eastern Front. This plan failed when the advance on Paris was halted by the French and British at the Battle of the Marne. At the subsequent Battle of the Aisne, neither side was able to gain an advantage, and the Germans began to dig substantial trenches on the high ground above the river, with the French and British having to follow suit. The line east of the battlefield had already settled and so both armies began a series of attempted outflanking movements, designed to infiltrate the rear areas and roll up the opposing front lines. In fact, this "Race to the Sea" merely extended the stalemate.

In what became known as the First Battle of Ypres, both sides unleashed a brutal series of frontal attacks in an attempt to break through, but all were unsuccessful. By Christmas 1914, the trench stalemate had become complete, and the lines of opposing trenches ran from the Belgian coast to the Swiss border.

The stalemate was particularly frustrating for the French military, who had been unable to clear their territory of the invading German army, but commanders on all sides were exasperated by this static form of warfare which none had expected or planned for. The British commander, Field Marshall Sir John French, said, "How I should love to have a real good 'go' at them in the open with lots of cavalry and horse artillery and run them to earth." Accordingly, between 1915 and 1917 the British and French forces mounted many offensives that aimed to break through the German defensive systems, reach open country and resume a war of movement. These offensives differed in their details and in their scale but most of them shared the same key elements; a massive preliminary artillery barrage to destroy enemy barbed wire, trench systems and communications, followed by an infantry assault in massed ranks designed to capture the destroyed positions and enable the next wave to advance beyond them.

In fact, these offensives achieved little. Often the bombardments did not destroy everything they were supposed to, and simply provided advance warning that an offensive was imminent, while German troops survived, safe in underground bunkers. The frontal assaults against German forces who remained in numbers were fearfully costly. After four and a half months of the Battle of the Somme in 1916, nowhere had the British pushed forward more than seven miles. The breakthrough and the return to mobile warfare remained elusive.

The Germans, on the other hand, mounted few offensives during the 1915–1917 period. The two main exceptions were the Second Battle of Ypres in 1915 and the 1916 Verdun campaign. It was in the former that poison gas, one of the earliest technological developments designed to break the deadlock, was first used. In general, though, the Germans focused on the defensive, strengthening their trench systems to make it ever more difficult for the Allies to break through. Most of Belgium and a large part of northern France lay in German hands and if they could be retained then Germany was in a strong bargaining position. As a result, German defences were usually more solid and extensive than the Allied ones. British soldiers who captured German trenches were often amazed at the large, comfortable, spacious dugouts they found that had survived the preliminary bombardment.

In 1917, along a stretch of the Western Front in the British sector running approximately from Arras to Soissons, the Germans retreated to prepared position the British came to call the Hindenburg Line, after the chief of the German general staff. In fact, the name applied by the Germans themselves was the Siegfried Stellung, or Siegfried Position. This was an exceptionally strong fortified system that made use of tunnels and canals and other landscape features. Trench systems elsewhere were also becoming more elaborate, based on defence in depth with more lines of trenches, thicker barbed wire and concrete bunkers and strongpoints. Yet eighteen months after the retreat to the Hindenburg Line, the breakthrough had been made and the war was over. How did this come about?

In retrospect, the unsuccessful Allied offensives of 1915–1917 appear to many as futile wastes of lives. However, some military historians have argued that Allied commanders learned a great deal from them, and that in due course they developed new techniques which increased the possibility of breaking through the German lines. Certainly, the Allied offensives successively introduced new methods, such as employing tanks and improved artillery techniques, but it is still a bitterly contested debate regarding how much Allied commanders had learned, and how much they were in control of affairs. Eventually, it was not the Allied powers who made the first breakthrough, but the Germans.

In the spring and early summer of 1918, the Germans launched a series of offensives on the Western Front. Suffering from the Royal Navy's North Sea blockade, and with the prospect of growing numbers of American troops critically tipping the balance on the Western Front, these offensives were very much Germany's last throw. The British and French front lines crumbled, their armies were forced to retreat, and a war of movement resumed, with the Allies fearing that Paris or the channel ports might again be in danger as they had appeared to be in 1914.

In fact, the breakthrough was not decisive. Paris did not fall, the front lines stabilized again and, from August to November, the Allies mounted a series of attacks that led to a continuous advance of a kind not seen since 1914. What had changed that, after years of stalemate, allowed the front lines to be broken?

New infantry methods were being widely adopted, with soldiers attacking in small groups instead of long lines, and focusing on weak points in the enemy line rather than the places of heaviest resistance. Artillery techniques became more sophisticated, with bombardments shorter and focused on specific targets. "Creeping" barrages continued during the attack, ahead of the advancing infantry and providing them with cover. Aircraft and tanks were also integrated into assault plans, though the Germans made surprisingly little use of tanks.

After the failure of the German spring offensives, with American troops flooding into the line and Britain and France drawing on the manpower resources of their empires, the Germans were becoming badly outnumbered on the Western Front. In addition, the troops available to them were much weaker. All the same, the fighting during the Allied advance remained fiercely contested and losses were at least as high on both sides as during the offensives of the static years 1915–17.

These developing new methods of warfare meant that the prolonged deadlock of the Western Front was never to be repeated. Nevertheless, this 450-mile linear battlefield, which was a scene of both unimaginable horror and extreme bravery, was a defining experience in the lives of millions, including, of course, Charles Horton.

NOTES

1. In England, a Nonconformist is a member of a Protestant church which dissents from the established Church of England. The roots of Nonconformity lie in the opposition to state interference in religious matters.
2. Within Methodism a circuit is a group of churches served by a team of ministers and local preachers. It is regarded as the primary way in which local churches express and experience their interconnection in the wider church.
3. "First line" defined the volunteer as prepared to serve overseas.
4. A "hussif" (shortened from "housewife") is a small sewing kit that was issued to soldiers.
5. Dover's powder was a traditional medicine used to fight cold and fever.
6. Within the Methodist Church, circuit stewards are lay people appointed by a circuit to be responsible with the superintendent and circuit ministers for the spiritual and material well-being of the circuit.